MW01074677

PRESENTED

TO

BY

ON

NIV
PSALMS
&
PROVERBS

ZONDERVAN

NIV Psalms and Proverbs
Copyright © 2018 by Zondervan

Published by Zondervan
3900 Sparks Dr. SE, Grand Rapids, Michigan 49546
All rights reserved

Library of Congress Catalog Card Number 2018938115

Printed in China

N120712

18 19 20 21 22 23 24 25 /AMC/ 20 19 18 17 16 15 14 13 12 11 10 9 8 7 6 5 4 3 2

A portion of the purchase price of your NIV® Bible is provided to Biblica so together we support the mission of *Transforming lives through God's Word.*

Biblica provides God's Word to people through translation, publishing and Bible engagement in Africa, Asia Pacific, Europe, Latin America, Middle East, and North America. Through its worldwide reach, Biblica engages people with God's Word so that their lives are transformed through a relationship with Jesus Christ.

PREFACE

The goal of the New International Version (NIV) is to enable English-speaking people from around the world to read and hear God's eternal Word in their own language. Our work as translators is motivated by our conviction that the Bible is God's Word in written form. We believe that the Bible contains the divine answer to the deepest needs of humanity, sheds unique light on our path in a dark world and sets forth the way to our eternal well-being. Out of these deep convictions, we have sought to recreate as far as possible the experience of the original audience — blending transparency to the original text with accessibility for the millions of English speakers around the world. We have prioritized accuracy, clarity and literary quality with the goal of creating a translation suitable for public and private reading, evangelism, teaching, preaching, memorizing and liturgical use. We have also sought to preserve a measure of continuity with the long tradition of translating the Scriptures into English.

The complete NIV Bible was first published in 1978. It was a completely new translation made by over a hundred scholars working directly from the best available Hebrew, Aramaic and Greek texts. The translators came from the United States, Great Britain, Canada, Australia and New Zealand, giving the translation an international scope. They were from many denominations and churches — including Anglican, Assemblies of God, Baptist, Brethren, Christian Reformed, Church of Christ, Evangelical Covenant, Evangelical Free, Lutheran, Mennonite, Methodist, Nazarene, Presbyterian, Wesleyan and others. This breadth of denominational and theological perspective helped to safeguard the translation from sectarian bias. For these reasons, and by the grace of God, the NIV has gained a wide readership in all parts of the English-speaking world.

The work of translating the Bible is never finished. As good as they are, English translations must be regularly updated so that they will continue to communicate accurately the meaning of God's Word. Updates are needed in order to reflect the latest developments in our understanding of the biblical world and its languages and to keep pace with changes in English usage. Recognizing, then, that the NIV would retain its ability to communicate God's Word accurately only if it were regularly updated, the original translators established the Committee on Bible Translation (CBT). The Committee is a self-perpetuating group of biblical scholars charged with keeping abreast of advances in biblical scholarship and changes in English and issuing periodic updates to the NIV. The CBT is an independent, self-governing body and has sole responsibility for the NIV text. The Committee mirrors the original group of translators in its diverse international and denominational makeup and in its unifying commitment to the Bible as God's inspired Word.

In obedience to its mandate, the Committee has issued periodic updates to the NIV. An initial revision was released in 1984. A more thorough revision process was completed in 2005, resulting in the separately published TNIV. The updated NIV you now have in your hands builds on both the original NIV and the TNIV and represents the latest effort of the Committee to articulate God's unchanging Word in the way the original authors might have said it had they been speaking in English to the global English-speaking audience today.

TRANSLATION PHILOSOPHY

The Committee's translating work has been governed by three widely accepted principles about the way people use words and about the way we understand them.

First, the meaning of words is determined by the way that users of the language actually use them at any given time. For the biblical languages, therefore, the Committee utilizes the best and most recent scholarship on the way Hebrew, Aramaic and Greek words were being used in biblical times. At the same time, the Committee carefully studies the state of modern English. Good translation is like good communication: one must know the target audience so that the appropriate choices can be made about which English words to use to represent the original words of Scripture. From its inception, the NIV has had as its target the general English-speaking population all over the world, the "International" in its title reflecting this concern. The aim of the Committee is to put the Scriptures into natural English that will communicate effectively with the broadest possible audience of English speakers.

Modern technology has enhanced the Committee's ability to choose the right English words to convey the meaning of the original text. The field of computational linguistics harnesses the power of computers to provide broadly applicable and current data about the state of the language. Translators can now access huge databases of modern English to better understand the current meaning and usage of key words. The Committee utilized this resource in preparing the 2011 edition of the NIV. An area of especially rapid and significant change in English is the way certain nouns and pronouns are used to refer to human beings. The Committee therefore requested experts in computational linguistics at Collins Dictionaries to pose some key questions about this usage to its database of English — the largest in the world, with over 4.4 billion words, gathered from several English-speaking countries and including both spoken and written English. (The Collins Study, called "The Development and Use of Gender Language in Contemporary English," can be accessed at *http://www.thenivbible.com/about-the-niv/about-the-2011-edition/*.) The study revealed that the most popular words to describe the human race in modern U.S. English were "humanity," "man" and "mankind." The Committee then used this data in the updated NIV, choosing from among these three words (and occasionally others also) depending on the context.

A related issue creates a larger problem for modern translations: the move away from using the third-person masculine singular pronouns — "he/him/his" — to refer to men and women equally. This usage does persist in some forms of English, and this revision therefore occasionally uses these pronouns in a generic sense. But the tendency, recognized in day-to-day usage and confirmed by the Collins study, is away from the generic use of "he," "him" and "his." In recognition of this shift in language and in an effort to translate into the natural English that people are actually using, this revision of the NIV generally uses other constructions when the biblical text is plainly addressed to men and women equally. The reader will encounter especially frequently a "they," "their" or "them" to express a generic singular idea. Thus, for instance, Mark 8:36 reads: "What good is it for someone to gain the whole world, yet forfeit their soul?" This generic use of the "distributive" or "singular" "they/them/their" has been used for many centuries by respected writers of English and has now become established as standard English, spoken and written, all over the world.

A second linguistic principle that feeds into the Committee's translation work is that meaning is found not in individual words, as vital as they are, but in larger clusters: phrases, clauses, sentences, discourses. Translation is not, as many people think, a matter of word substitution: English word *x* in place of Hebrew word *y*. Translators must first determine the meaning of the words of the biblical languages in the context of the passage and then select English words that accurately communicate that meaning to modern listeners and readers. This means that accurate translation will not always reflect the exact structure of the original language. To be sure, there is debate over the degree to which translators should try to preserve the "form" of the original text in English. From the beginning, the NIV has taken a mediating position on this issue. The manual produced when the translation that became the NIV was first being planned states: "If the Greek or Hebrew syntax has a good parallel in modern English, it should be used. But if there is no good parallel, the English syntax appropriate to the meaning of the original is to be chosen."

It is fine, in other words, to carry over the form of the biblical languages into English — but not at the expense of natural expression. The principle that meaning resides in larger clusters of words means that the Committee has not insisted on a "word-for-word" approach to translation. We certainly believe that every word of Scripture is inspired by God and therefore to be carefully studied to determine what God is saying to us. It is for this reason that the Committee labors over every single word of the original texts, working hard to determine how each of those words contributes to what the text is saying. Ultimately, however, it is how these individual words function in combination with other words that determines meaning.

A third linguistic principle guiding the Committee in its translation work is the recognition that words have a spectrum of meaning. It is popular to define a word by using another word, or "gloss," to substitute for it. This substitute word is then sometimes called the "literal" meaning of a word. In fact, however, words have a range of possible meanings. Those meanings will vary depending on the context, and words in one language will usually not occupy the same semantic range as words in another language. The Committee therefore studies each original word of Scripture in its context to identify its meaning in a particular verse and then chooses an appropriate English word (or phrase) to represent it. It is impossible, then, to translate any given Hebrew, Aramaic or Greek word with the same English word all the time. The Committee does try to translate related occurrences of a word in the original languages with the same English word in order to preserve the connection for the English reader. But the Committee generally privileges clear natural meaning over a concern with consistency in rendering particular words.

TEXTUAL BASIS

For the Old Testament the standard Hebrew text, the Masoretic Text as published in the latest edition of *Biblia Hebraica*, has been used throughout. The Masoretic Text tradition contains marginal notations that offer variant readings. These have sometimes been followed instead of the text itself. Because such instances involve variants within the Masoretic tradition, they have not been indicated in the textual notes. In a few cases, words in the basic consonantal text have been divided differently than in the Masoretic Text. Such cases are usually indicated in the textual footnotes. The Dead Sea Scrolls contain biblical texts that represent an earlier stage of the transmission of the Hebrew text. They have been consulted, as have been the Samaritan Pentateuch and the ancient scribal traditions concerning deliberate textual changes. The translators also consulted the more important early versions. Readings from these versions, the Dead Sea Scrolls and the scribal traditions were occasionally followed where the Masoretic Text seemed doubtful and where accepted principles of textual criticism showed that one or more of these textual witnesses appeared to provide the correct reading. In rare cases, the translators have emended the Hebrew text where it appears to have become corrupted at an even earlier stage of its transmission. These departures from the Masoretic Text are also indicated in the textual footnotes. Sometimes the vowel indicators (which are later additions to the basic consonantal text) found in the Masoretic Text did not, in the judgment of the translators, represent the correct vowels for the original text. Accordingly, some words have been read with a different set of vowels. These instances are usually not indicated in the footnotes.

The Greek text used in translating the New Testament has been an eclectic one, based on the latest editions of the Nestle-Aland/United Bible Societies' Greek New Testament. The translators have made their choices among the variant readings in accordance with widely accepted principles of New Testament textual criticism. Footnotes call attention to places where uncertainty remains.

The New Testament authors, writing in Greek, often quote the Old Testament from its ancient Greek version, the Septuagint. This is one reason why some of the Old Testament quotations in the NIV New Testament are not identical to the corresponding passages in the NIV Old Testament. Such quotations in the New Testament are indicated with the footnote "(see Septuagint)."

FOOTNOTES AND FORMATTING

Footnotes in this version are of several kinds, most of which need no explanation. Those giving alternative translations begin with "Or" and generally introduce the alternative with the last word preceding it in the text, except when it is a single-word alternative. When poetry is quoted in a footnote a slash mark indicates a line division.

It should be noted that references to diseases, minerals, flora and fauna, architectural details, clothing, jewelry, musical instruments and other articles cannot always be identified with precision. Also, linear measurements and measures of capacity can only be approximated (see the Table of Weights and Measures). Although *Selah*, used mainly in the Psalms, is probably a musical term, its meaning is uncertain. Since it may interrupt reading and distract the reader, this word has not been kept in the English text, but every occurrence has been signaled by a footnote.

As an aid to the reader, sectional headings have been inserted. They are not to be regarded as part of the biblical text and are not intended for oral reading. It is the Committee's hope that these headings may prove more helpful to the reader than the traditional chapter divisions, which were introduced long after the Bible was written.

Sometimes the chapter and/or verse numbering in English translations of the Old Testament differs from that found in published Hebrew texts. This is particularly the case in the Psalms, where the traditional titles are included in the Hebrew verse numbering. Such differences are indicated in the footnotes at the bottom of the page. In the New Testament, verse numbers that marked off portions of the traditional English text not supported by the best Greek manuscripts now appear in brackets, with a footnote indicating the text that has been omitted (see, for example, Matthew 17:[21]).

Mark 16:9 – 20 and John 7:53 — 8:11, although long accorded virtually equal status with the rest of the Gospels in which they stand, have a questionable standing in the textual history of the New Testament, as noted in the bracketed annotations with which they are set off. A different typeface has been chosen for these passages to indicate their uncertain status.

Basic formatting of the text, such as lining the poetry, paragraphing (both prose and poetry), setting up of (administrative-like) lists, indenting letters and lengthy prayers within narratives and the insertion of sectional headings, has been the work of the Committee. However, the choice between single-column and double-column formats has been left to the publishers. Also the issuing of "red-letter" editions is a publisher's choice — one that the Committee does not endorse.

The Committee has again been reminded that every human effort is flawed — including this revision of the NIV. We trust, however, that many will find in it an improved representation of the Word of God, through which they hear his call to faith in our Lord Jesus Christ and to service in his kingdom. We offer this version of the Bible to him in whose name and for whose glory it has been made.

The Committee on Bible Translation

PSALMS

WHAT IS A PSALM?

The book of Psalms is just one of sixty-six books of the Holy Bible. The psalms are part of the Old Testament of the Bible. The book of Psalms is divided into five sections, each closing with a benediction, a kind of prayer. The word *psalm* comes from a Greek word meaning "instrumental music" and specifically relates to the words accompanying the music. So, the book of Psalms is a collection of 150 individual lyrics to old Hebrew songs. Many of the psalms were thought to be written by the Hebrew king David, but we cannot know that for sure. What we can know is that whoever the authors were, each was empowered by God to write these words.

But what are psalms? Psalms are poems. Unlike other parts of the Bible, they don't preach or tell a story or prophesy. They use figurative language to either praise God, thank God or express deep emotion. Psalms are also songs. The Hebrew title of the book of Psalms is *Tehillim*, which means "songs of praise," and many of the psalms note that they are for the "Director of Music."

And why are the psalms important? Psalms are tools of worship and praise. The writers of the psalms used them to express their emotions about their circumstances, to praise God and to thank God for his wonderful gifts. The psalms are another way for us to interact with the God of our hearts through the power of his Word.

BOOK I

Psalms 1–41

PSALM 1

1   Blessed is the one
        who does not walk in step with the wicked
    or stand in the way that sinners take
        or sit in the company of mockers,
2   but whose delight is in the law of the LORD,
        and who meditates on his law day and night.
3   That person is like a tree planted by streams
            of water,
        which yields its fruit in season
    and whose leaf does not wither —
        whatever they do prospers.

4   Not so the wicked!
        They are like chaff
        that the wind blows away.
5   Therefore the wicked will not stand in the
            judgment,
        nor sinners in the assembly of the righteous.

6   For the LORD watches over the way of the
            righteous,
        but the way of the wicked leads to
            destruction.

PSALM 2

1   Why do the nations conspire
        and the peoples plot in vain?
2   The kings of the earth rise up
        and the rulers band together
        against the Lord and against his anointed,
           saying,
3   "Let us break their chains
        and throw off their shackles."

4   The One enthroned in heaven laughs;
        the Lord scoffs at them.
5   He rebukes them in his anger
        and terrifies them in his wrath, saying,
6   "I have installed my king
        on Zion, my holy mountain."

7   I will proclaim the Lord's decree:

        He said to me, "You are my son;
        today I have become your father.
8   Ask me,
        and I will make the nations your
           inheritance,
        the ends of the earth your possession.
9   You will break them with a rod of iron;
        you will dash them to pieces like pottery."

10   Therefore, you kings, be wise;
        be warned, you rulers of the earth.

11 Serve the Lord with fear
   and celebrate his rule with trembling.
12 Kiss his son, or he will be angry
   and your way will lead to your destruction,
  for his wrath can flare up in a moment.
   Blessed are all who take refuge in him.

PSALM 3

*A psalm of David. When he fled
from his son Absalom.*

1   Lord, how many are my foes!
      How many rise up against me!
2   Many are saying of me,
      "God will not deliver him."

3   But you, Lord, are a shield around me,
      my glory, the One who lifts my head high.
4   I call out to the Lord,
      and he answers me from his holy mountain.

5   I lie down and sleep;
      I wake again, because the Lord sustains me.
6   I will not fear though tens of thousands
      assail me on every side.

7   Arise, Lord!
      Deliver me, my God!
   Strike all my enemies on the jaw;
      break the teeth of the wicked.

8   From the Lord comes deliverance.
      May your blessing be on your people.

PSALM 4

For the director of music. With stringed instruments. A psalm of David.

1 Answer me when I call to you,
    my righteous God.
  Give me relief from my distress;
    have mercy on me and hear my
        prayer.

2 How long will you people turn my glory into
        shame?
    How long will you love delusions and seek
        false gods?

3 Know that the LORD has set apart his faithful
        servant for himself;
    the LORD hears when I call to him.

4 Tremble and do not sin;
    when you are on your beds,
    search your hearts and be silent.

5 Offer the sacrifices of the righteous
    and trust in the LORD.

6 Many, LORD, are asking, "Who will bring us
        prosperity?"
    Let the light of your face shine on us.

7 Fill my heart with joy
    when their grain and new wine
        abound.

8   In peace I will lie down and sleep,
      for you alone, LORD,
      make me dwell in safety.

PSALM 5

For the director of music. For pipes.
A psalm of David.

1   Listen to my words, LORD,
  consider my lament.
2   Hear my cry for help,
  my King and my God,
  for to you I pray.

3   In the morning, LORD, you hear my voice;
  in the morning I lay my requests before you
  and wait expectantly.
4   For you are not a God who is pleased with
    wickedness;
  with you, evil people are not welcome.
5   The arrogant cannot stand
  in your presence.
You hate all who do wrong;
6   you destroy those who tell lies.
The bloodthirsty and deceitful
  you, LORD, detest.
7   But I, by your great love,
  can come into your house;
in reverence I bow down
  toward your holy temple.

8   Lead me, LORD, in your righteousness
  because of my enemies —
  make your way straight before me.

9 Not a word from their mouth can be trusted;
      their heart is filled with malice.
   Their throat is an open grave;
      with their tongues they tell lies.
10 Declare them guilty, O God!
      Let their intrigues be their downfall.
   Banish them for their many sins,
      for they have rebelled against you.
11 But let all who take refuge in you be glad;
      let them ever sing for joy.
   Spread your protection over them,
      that those who love your name may rejoice
         in you.

12 Surely, Lord, you bless the righteous;
      you surround them with your favor as with a
         shield.

PSALM 6

For the director of music. With stringed instruments.
According to sheminith. *A psalm of David.*

1 LORD, do not rebuke me in your anger
    or discipline me in your wrath.
2 Have mercy on me, LORD, for I am faint;
    heal me, LORD, for my bones are in agony.
3 My soul is in deep anguish.
    How long, LORD, how long?

4 Turn, LORD, and deliver me;
    save me because of your unfailing love.
5 Among the dead no one proclaims your name.
    Who praises you from the grave?

6 I am worn out from my groaning.

    All night long I flood my bed with weeping
    and drench my couch with tears.
7 My eyes grow weak with sorrow;
    they fail because of all my foes.

8 Away from me, all you who do evil,
    for the LORD has heard my weeping.
9 The LORD has heard my cry for mercy;
    the LORD accepts my prayer.
10 All my enemies will be overwhelmed with
    shame and anguish;
    they will turn back and suddenly be put to
    shame.

PSALM 7

A shiggaion *of David, which he sang to the*
LORD *concerning Cush, a Benjamite.*

1 LORD my God, I take refuge in you;
    save and deliver me from all who pursue me,
2 or they will tear me apart like a lion
    and rip me to pieces with no one to
        rescue me.

3 LORD my God, if I have done this
    and there is guilt on my hands —
4 if I have repaid my ally with evil
    or without cause have robbed my foe —
5 then let my enemy pursue and overtake me;
    let him trample my life to the ground
    and make me sleep in the dust.

6 Arise, LORD, in your anger;
    rise up against the rage of my enemies.
    Awake, my God; decree justice.
7 Let the assembled peoples gather around you,
    while you sit enthroned over them on
        high.
8 Let the LORD judge the peoples.
Vindicate me, LORD, according to my
        righteousness,
    according to my integrity, O Most High.
9 Bring to an end the violence of the wicked
    and make the righteous secure —

you, the righteous God
   who probes minds and hearts.

10   My shield is God Most High,
         who saves the upright in heart.
11   God is a righteous judge,
         a God who displays his wrath every day.
12   If he does not relent,
         he will sharpen his sword;
         he will bend and string his bow.
13   He has prepared his deadly weapons;
         he makes ready his flaming arrows.

14   Whoever is pregnant with evil
         conceives trouble and gives birth to
            disillusionment.
15   Whoever digs a hole and scoops it out
         falls into the pit they have made.
16   The trouble they cause recoils on them;
         their violence comes down on their own
            heads.

17   I will give thanks to the LORD because of his
            righteousness;
         I will sing the praises of the name of the
            LORD Most High.

PSALM 8

*For the director of music. According
to* gittith. *A psalm of David.*

1 LORD, our Lord,
    how majestic is your name in all the
        earth!

   You have set your glory
       in the heavens.
2 Through the praise of children and infants
       you have established a stronghold against
           your enemies,
       to silence the foe and the avenger.
3 When I consider your heavens,
       the work of your fingers,
   the moon and the stars,
       which you have set in place,
4 what is mankind that you are mindful of
           them,
       human beings that you care for them?

5 You have made them a little lower than the
           angels
       and crowned them with glory and honor.
6 You made them rulers over the works of
           your hands;
       you put everything under their feet:
7 all flocks and herds,
       and the animals of the wild,

8   the birds in the sky,
           and the fish in the sea,
           all that swim the paths of the seas.

9   LORD, our Lord,
           how majestic is your name in all the earth!

PSALM 9

For the director of music. To the tune of "The Death of the Son." A psalm of David.

1   I will give thanks to you, LORD, with all my
          heart;
      I will tell of all your wonderful deeds.
2   I will be glad and rejoice in you;
      I will sing the praises of your name,
          O Most High.

3   My enemies turn back;
      they stumble and perish before you.
4   For you have upheld my right and my
          cause,
      sitting enthroned as the righteous judge.
5   You have rebuked the nations and destroyed
          the wicked;
      you have blotted out their name for ever
          and ever.
6   Endless ruin has overtaken my enemies,
      you have uprooted their cities;
      even the memory of them has perished.

7   The LORD reigns forever;
      he has established his throne for judgment.
8   He rules the world in righteousness
      and judges the peoples with equity.
9   The LORD is a refuge for the oppressed,
      a stronghold in times of trouble.

10   Those who know your name trust in you,
        for you, Lord, have never forsaken those
            who seek you.

11   Sing the praises of the Lord, enthroned in
            Zion;
        proclaim among the nations what he has done.
12   For he who avenges blood remembers;
        he does not ignore the cries of the afflicted.

13   Lord, see how my enemies persecute me!
        Have mercy and lift me up from the gates of
            death,
14   that I may declare your praises
        in the gates of Daughter Zion,
        and there rejoice in your salvation.

15   The nations have fallen into the pit they have
            dug;
        their feet are caught in the net they have
            hidden.
16   The Lord is known by his acts of justice;
        the wicked are ensnared by the work of their
            hands.
17   The wicked go down to the realm of the dead,
        all the nations that forget God.
18   But God will never forget the needy;
        the hope of the afflicted will never perish.

19   Arise, Lord, do not let mortals triumph;
        let the nations be judged in your presence.
20   Strike them with terror, Lord;
        let the nations know they are only mortal.

PSALM 10

1   Why, LORD, do you stand far off?
     Why do you hide yourself in times of
         trouble?

2   In his arrogance the wicked man hunts down
         the weak,
     who are caught in the schemes he devises.

3   He boasts about the cravings of his heart;
     he blesses the greedy and reviles the LORD.

4   In his pride the wicked man does not seek
         him;
     in all his thoughts there is no room for God.

5   His ways are always prosperous;
     your laws are rejected by him;
     he sneers at all his enemies.

6   He says to himself, "Nothing will ever
         shake me."
     He swears, "No one will ever do me harm."

7   His mouth is full of lies and threats;
     trouble and evil are under his tongue.

8   He lies in wait near the villages;
     from ambush he murders the innocent.
     His eyes watch in secret for his victims;

9   like a lion in cover he lies in wait.
     He lies in wait to catch the helpless;
     he catches the helpless and drags them off in
         his net.

10   His victims are crushed, they collapse;
     they fall under his strength.
11   He says to himself, "God will never notice;
     he covers his face and never sees."

12   Arise, Lord! Lift up your hand, O God.
     Do not forget the helpless.
13   Why does the wicked man revile God?
     Why does he say to himself,
     "He won't call me to account"?
14   But you, God, see the trouble of the afflicted;
     you consider their grief and take it in hand.
The victims commit themselves to you;
     you are the helper of the fatherless.
15   Break the arm of the wicked man;
     call the evildoer to account for his
          wickedness
     that would not otherwise be found out.

16   The Lord is King for ever and ever;
     the nations will perish from his land.
17   You, Lord, hear the desire of the afflicted;
     you encourage them, and you listen to
          their cry,
18   defending the fatherless and the oppressed,
     so that mere earthly mortals
     will never again strike terror.

PSALM 11

For the director of music. Of David.

1 In the LORD I take refuge.
  How then can you say to me:
  "Flee like a bird to your mountain.
2 For look, the wicked bend their bows;
  they set their arrows against the strings
to shoot from the shadows
  at the upright in heart.
3 When the foundations are being destroyed,
  what can the righteous do?"

4 The LORD is in his holy temple;
  the LORD is on his heavenly throne.
He observes everyone on earth;
  his eyes examine them.
5 The LORD examines the righteous,
  but the wicked, those who love violence,
  he hates with a passion.
6 On the wicked he will rain
  fiery coals and burning sulfur;
  a scorching wind will be their lot.

7 For the LORD is righteous,
  he loves justice;
  the upright will see his face.

PSALM 12

*For the director of music. According
to* sheminith. *A psalm of David.*

1 Help, LORD, for no one is faithful anymore;
    those who are loyal have vanished from the
        human race.
2 Everyone lies to their neighbor;
    they flatter with their lips
    but harbor deception in their hearts.

3 May the LORD silence all flattering lips
    and every boastful tongue —
4 those who say,
    "By our tongues we will prevail;
    our own lips will defend us — who is lord
        over us?"

5 "Because the poor are plundered and the
        needy groan,
    I will now arise," says the LORD.
    "I will protect them from those who malign
        them."
6 And the words of the LORD are flawless,
    like silver purified in a crucible,
    like gold refined seven times.

7 You, LORD, will keep the needy safe
    and will protect us forever from the
        wicked,

8   who freely strut about
       when what is vile is honored by the human
          race.

PSALM 13

For the director of music. A psalm of David.

1 How long, LORD? Will you forget me forever?
   How long will you hide your face from me?
2 How long must I wrestle with my thoughts
   and day after day have sorrow in my heart?
   How long will my enemy triumph over me?

3 Look on me and answer, LORD my God.
   Give light to my eyes, or I will sleep in death,
4 and my enemy will say, "I have overcome him,"
   and my foes will rejoice when I fall.

5 But I trust in your unfailing love;
   my heart rejoices in your salvation.
6 I will sing the LORD's praise,
   for he has been good to me.

PSALM 14

For the director of music. Of David.

1 The fool says in his heart,
   "There is no God."
   They are corrupt, their deeds are vile;
   there is no one who does good.

2 The LORD looks down from heaven
   on all mankind
   to see if there are any who understand,
   any who seek God.

3 All have turned away, all have become corrupt;
   there is no one who does good,
   not even one.

4 Do all these evildoers know nothing?

   They devour my people as though eating
   bread;
   they never call on the LORD.

5 But there they are, overwhelmed with dread,
   for God is present in the company of the
   righteous.

6 You evildoers frustrate the plans of the poor,
   but the LORD is their refuge.

7 Oh, that salvation for Israel would come out of
   Zion!
   When the LORD restores his people,
   let Jacob rejoice and Israel be glad!

PSALM 15

A psalm of David.

1   LORD, who may dwell in your sacred tent?
       Who may live on your holy mountain?

2   The one whose walk is blameless,
       who does what is righteous,
       who speaks the truth from their heart;
3   whose tongue utters no slander,
       who does no wrong to a neighbor,
       and casts no slur on others;
4   who despises a vile person
       but honors those who fear the LORD;
       who keeps an oath even when it hurts,
       and does not change their mind;
5   who lends money to the poor without interest;
       who does not accept a bribe against the
         innocent.

     Whoever does these things
       will never be shaken.

PSALM 16

A miktam of David.

1   Keep me safe, my God,
        for in you I take refuge.

2   I say to the LORD, "You are my Lord;
        apart from you I have no good thing."

3   I say of the holy people who are in the land,
        "They are the noble ones in whom is all my
            delight."

4   Those who run after other gods will suffer
            more and more.
        I will not pour out libations of blood to such
            gods
        or take up their names on my lips.

5   LORD, you alone are my portion and my cup;
        you make my lot secure.

6   The boundary lines have fallen for me in
            pleasant places;
        surely I have a delightful inheritance.

7   I will praise the LORD, who counsels me;
        even at night my heart instructs me.

8   I keep my eyes always on the LORD.
        With him at my right hand, I will not be
            shaken.

9   Therefore my heart is glad and my tongue
            rejoices;
        my body also will rest secure,

10   because you will not abandon me to the realm
             of the dead,
        nor will you let your faithful one see decay.
11   You make known to me the path of life;
        you will fill me with joy in your presence,
        with eternal pleasures at your right
            hand.

PSALM 17

A prayer of David.

1   Hear me, Lord, my plea is just;
        listen to my cry.
    Hear my prayer—
        it does not rise from deceitful lips.
2   Let my vindication come from you;
        may your eyes see what is right.

3   Though you probe my heart,
        though you examine me at night and
            test me,
    you will find that I have planned no evil;
        my mouth has not transgressed.
4   Though people tried to bribe me,
        I have kept myself from the ways of the
            violent
        through what your lips have commanded.
5   My steps have held to your paths;
        my feet have not stumbled.

6   I call on you, my God, for you will answer me;
        turn your ear to me and hear my prayer.
7   Show me the wonders of your great love,
        you who save by your right hand
        those who take refuge in you from their
            foes.
8   Keep me as the apple of your eye;
        hide me in the shadow of your wings

9   from the wicked who are out to destroy me,
       from my mortal enemies who surround me.

10   They close up their callous hearts,
       and their mouths speak with arrogance.

11   They have tracked me down, they now
        surround me,
       with eyes alert, to throw me to the ground.

12   They are like a lion hungry for prey,
       like a fierce lion crouching in cover.

13   Rise up, LORD, confront them, bring them
        down;
       with your sword rescue me from the
        wicked.

14   By your hand save me from such people, LORD,
       from those of this world whose reward is in
        this life.
    May what you have stored up for the wicked fill
       their bellies;
       may their children gorge themselves on it,
       and may there be leftovers for their little
        ones.

15   As for me, I will be vindicated and will see your
        face;
       when I awake, I will be satisfied with seeing
        your likeness.

PSALM 18

For the director of music. Of David the servant of the
LORD. He sang to the LORD the words of this song
when the LORD delivered him from the hand of all
his enemies and from the hand of Saul. He said:

1   I love you, LORD, my strength.

2   The LORD is my rock, my fortress and my
            deliverer;
      my God is my rock, in whom I take
            refuge,
      my shield and the horn of my salvation,
            my stronghold.

3   I called to the LORD, who is worthy of praise,
      and I have been saved from my enemies.
4   The cords of death entangled me;
      the torrents of destruction overwhelmed me.
5   The cords of the grave coiled around me;
      the snares of death confronted me.

6   In my distress I called to the LORD;
      I cried to my God for help.
   From his temple he heard my voice;
      my cry came before him, into his
            ears.
7   The earth trembled and quaked,
      and the foundations of the mountains
            shook;
      they trembled because he was angry.

8 Smoke rose from his nostrils;
   consuming fire came from his mouth,
   burning coals blazed out of it.
9 He parted the heavens and came down;
   dark clouds were under his feet.
10 He mounted the cherubim and flew;
   he soared on the wings of the wind.
11 He made darkness his covering, his canopy
    around him —
   the dark rain clouds of the sky.
12 Out of the brightness of his presence clouds
    advanced,
   with hailstones and bolts of lightning.
13 The Lord thundered from heaven;
   the voice of the Most High resounded.
14 He shot his arrows and scattered the enemy,
   with great bolts of lightning he routed
    them.
15 The valleys of the sea were exposed
   and the foundations of the earth laid bare
  at your rebuke, Lord,
   at the blast of breath from your nostrils.

16 He reached down from on high and took hold
    of me;
   he drew me out of deep waters.
17 He rescued me from my powerful enemy,
   from my foes, who were too strong for me.
18 They confronted me in the day of my disaster,
   but the Lord was my support.
19 He brought me out into a spacious place;
   he rescued me because he delighted in me.

20 The LORD has dealt with me according to my
       righteousness;
     according to the cleanness of my hands he
       has rewarded me.
21 For I have kept the ways of the LORD;
     I am not guilty of turning from my God.
22 All his laws are before me;
     I have not turned away from his decrees.
23 I have been blameless before him
     and have kept myself from sin.
24 The LORD has rewarded me according to my
       righteousness,
     according to the cleanness of my hands in
       his sight.

25 To the faithful you show yourself faithful,
     to the blameless you show yourself
       blameless,
26 to the pure you show yourself pure,
     but to the devious you show yourself shrewd.
27 You save the humble
     but bring low those whose eyes are haughty.
28 You, LORD, keep my lamp burning;
     my God turns my darkness into light.
29 With your help I can advance against a troop;
     with my God I can scale a wall.

30 As for God, his way is perfect:
     The LORD's word is flawless;
     he shields all who take refuge in him.
31 For who is God besides the LORD?
     And who is the Rock except our God?

32 It is God who arms me with strength
and keeps my way secure.
33 He makes my feet like the feet of a deer;
he causes me to stand on the heights.
34 He trains my hands for battle;
my arms can bend a bow of bronze.
35 You make your saving help my shield,
and your right hand sustains me;
your help has made me great.
36 You provide a broad path for my feet,
so that my ankles do not give way.

37 I pursued my enemies and overtook them;
I did not turn back till they were destroyed.
38 I crushed them so that they could not rise;
they fell beneath my feet.
39 You armed me with strength for battle;
you humbled my adversaries before me.
40 You made my enemies turn their backs in
flight,
and I destroyed my foes.
41 They cried for help, but there was no one to
save them —
to the LORD, but he did not answer.
42 I beat them as fine as windblown dust;
I trampled them like mud in the streets.
43 You have delivered me from the attacks of the
people;
you have made me the head of nations.
People I did not know now serve me,
44 foreigners cower before me;
as soon as they hear of me, they obey me.

45   They all lose heart;
          they come trembling from their strongholds.

46   The Lord lives! Praise be to my Rock!
          Exalted be God my Savior!
47   He is the God who avenges me,
          who subdues nations under me,
48   who saves me from my enemies.
      You exalted me above my foes;
          from a violent man you rescued me.
49   Therefore I will praise you, Lord, among the
              nations;
          I will sing the praises of your name.

50   He gives his king great victories;
          he shows unfailing love to his anointed,
          to David and to his descendants forever.

PSALM 19

For the director of music. A psalm of David.

1 The heavens declare the glory of God;
    the skies proclaim the work of his hands.
2 Day after day they pour forth speech;
    night after night they reveal knowledge.
3 They have no speech, they use no words;
    no sound is heard from them.
4 Yet their voice goes out into all the earth,
    their words to the ends of the world.
In the heavens God has pitched a tent for
      the sun.
5   It is like a bridegroom coming out of his
      chamber,
    like a champion rejoicing to run his
      course.
6 It rises at one end of the heavens
    and makes its circuit to the other;
    nothing is deprived of its warmth.

7 The law of the LORD is perfect,
    refreshing the soul.
The statutes of the LORD are trustworthy,
    making wise the simple.
8 The precepts of the LORD are right,
    giving joy to the heart.
The commands of the LORD are radiant,
    giving light to the eyes.

9	The fear of the LORD is pure,
	enduring forever.
	The decrees of the LORD are firm,
	and all of them are righteous.

10	They are more precious than gold,
	than much pure gold;
	they are sweeter than honey,
	than honey from the honeycomb.

11	By them your servant is warned;
	in keeping them there is great reward.

12	But who can discern their own errors?
	Forgive my hidden faults.

13	Keep your servant also from willful sins;
	may they not rule over me.
	Then I will be blameless,
	innocent of great transgression.

14	May these words of my mouth and this
	meditation of my heart
	be pleasing in your sight,
	LORD, my Rock and my Redeemer.

PSALM 20

For the director of music. A psalm of David.

1   May the LORD answer you when you are in
        distress;
        may the name of the God of Jacob protect
        you.

2   May he send you help from the sanctuary
        and grant you support from Zion.

3   May he remember all your sacrifices
        and accept your burnt offerings.

4   May he give you the desire of your heart
        and make all your plans succeed.

5   May we shout for joy over your victory
        and lift up our banners in the name of
        our God.

May the LORD grant all your requests.

6   Now this I know:
        The LORD gives victory to his anointed.
    He answers him from his heavenly sanctuary
        with the victorious power of his right hand.

7   Some trust in chariots and some in horses,
        but we trust in the name of the LORD
        our God.

8   They are brought to their knees and fall,
        but we rise up and stand firm.

9   LORD, give victory to the king!
        Answer us when we call!

PSALM 21

For the director of music. A psalm of David.

1 The king rejoices in your strength, LORD.
    How great is his joy in the victories you give!

2 You have granted him his heart's desire
    and have not withheld the request of his
        lips.

3 You came to greet him with rich blessings
    and placed a crown of pure gold on his head.

4 He asked you for life, and you gave it to him —
    length of days, for ever and ever.

5 Through the victories you gave, his glory is
        great;
    you have bestowed on him splendor and
        majesty.

6 Surely you have granted him unending
        blessings
    and made him glad with the joy of your
        presence.

7 For the king trusts in the LORD;
    through the unfailing love of the Most High
    he will not be shaken.

8 Your hand will lay hold on all your enemies;
    your right hand will seize your foes.

9 When you appear for battle,
    you will burn them up as in a blazing
        furnace.

The LORD will swallow them up in his wrath,
and his fire will consume them.
10   You will destroy their descendants from the
earth,
their posterity from mankind.
11   Though they plot evil against you
and devise wicked schemes, they cannot
succeed.
12   You will make them turn their backs
when you aim at them with drawn bow.

13   Be exalted in your strength, LORD;
we will sing and praise your might.

PSALM 22

For the director of music. To the tune of "The Doe of the Morning." A psalm of David.

1   My God, my God, why have you forsaken me?
     Why are you so far from saving me,
      so far from my cries of anguish?
2   My God, I cry out by day, but you do not
      answer,
     by night, but I find no rest.

3   Yet you are enthroned as the Holy One;
     you are the one Israel praises.
4   In you our ancestors put their trust;
     they trusted and you delivered
      them.
5   To you they cried out and were saved;
     in you they trusted and were not put
      to shame.

6   But I am a worm and not a man,
     scorned by everyone, despised by the
      people.
7   All who see me mock me;
     they hurl insults, shaking their
      heads.
8   "He trusts in the LORD," they say,
     "let the LORD rescue him.
   Let him deliver him,
     since he delights in him."

9   Yet you brought me out of the
              womb;
          you made me trust in you, even
              at my mother's breast.
10 From birth I was cast on you;
          from my mother's womb you have
              been my God.

11 Do not be far from me,
          for trouble is near
          and there is no one to help.

12 Many bulls surround me;
          strong bulls of Bashan encircle me.
13 Roaring lions that tear their prey
          open their mouths wide against me.
14 I am poured out like water,
          and all my bones are out of joint.
      My heart has turned to wax;
          it has melted within me.
15 My mouth is dried up like a potsherd,
          and my tongue sticks to the roof of
              my mouth;
          you lay me in the dust of death.

16 Dogs surround me,
          a pack of villains encircles me;
          they pierce my hands and my feet.
17 All my bones are on display;
          people stare and gloat over me.
18 They divide my clothes among them
          and cast lots for my garment.

19 But you, LORD, do not be far from me.
   You are my strength; come quickly to
      help me.
20 Deliver me from the sword,
   my precious life from the power of the dogs.
21 Rescue me from the mouth of the lions;
   save me from the horns of the wild oxen.

22 I will declare your name to my people;
   in the assembly I will praise you.
23 You who fear the LORD, praise him!
   All you descendants of Jacob, honor him!
   Revere him, all you descendants of Israel!
24 For he has not despised or scorned
      the suffering of the afflicted one;
   he has not hidden his face from him
      but has listened to his cry for help.

25 From you comes the theme of my praise in the
      great assembly;
   before those who fear you I will fulfill my
      vows.
26 The poor will eat and be satisfied;
   those who seek the LORD will praise him —
      may your hearts live forever!

27 All the ends of the earth
      will remember and turn to the LORD,
   and all the families of the nations
      will bow down before him,
28 for dominion belongs to the LORD
   and he rules over the nations.

29 All the rich of the earth will feast and worship;
   all who go down to the dust will kneel before
      him —
   those who cannot keep themselves alive.
30 Posterity will serve him;
   future generations will be told about the
      Lord.
31 They will proclaim his righteousness,
   declaring to a people yet unborn:
   He has done it!

PSALM 23

A psalm of David.

1 The LORD is my shepherd, I lack nothing.
2   He makes me lie down in green pastures,
he leads me beside quiet waters,
3   he refreshes my soul.
He guides me along the right paths
    for his name's sake.
4 Even though I walk
    through the darkest valley,
I will fear no evil,
    for you are with me;
your rod and your staff,
    they comfort me.

5 You prepare a table before me
    in the presence of my enemies.
You anoint my head with oil;
    my cup overflows.
6 Surely your goodness and love will follow me
    all the days of my life,
and I will dwell in the house of the LORD
    forever.

PSALM 24

Of David. A psalm.

1 The earth is the LORD's, and everything in it,
    the world, and all who live in it;
2 for he founded it on the seas
    and established it on the waters.

3 Who may ascend the mountain of the LORD?
    Who may stand in his holy place?
4 The one who has clean hands and a pure heart,
    who does not trust in an idol
    or swear by a false god.

5 They will receive blessing from the LORD
    and vindication from God their Savior.
6 Such is the generation of those who seek him,
    who seek your face, God of Jacob.

7 Lift up your heads, you gates;
    be lifted up, you ancient doors,
    that the King of glory may come in.
8 Who is this King of glory?
    The LORD strong and mighty,
    the LORD mighty in battle.
9 Lift up your heads, you gates;
    lift them up, you ancient doors,
    that the King of glory may come in.
10 Who is he, this King of glory?
    The LORD Almighty—
    he is the King of glory.

PSALM 25

Of David.

1   In you, LORD my God,
       I put my trust.

2   I trust in you;
       do not let me be put to shame,
       nor let my enemies triumph over me.

3   No one who hopes in you
       will ever be put to shame,
   but shame will come on those
       who are treacherous without cause.

4   Show me your ways, LORD,
       teach me your paths.

5   Guide me in your truth and teach me,
       for you are God my Savior,
       and my hope is in you all day long.

6   Remember, LORD, your great mercy and love,
       for they are from of old.

7   Do not remember the sins of my youth
       and my rebellious ways;
   according to your love remember me,
       for you, LORD, are good.

8   Good and upright is the LORD;
       therefore he instructs sinners in his ways.

9   He guides the humble in what is right
       and teaches them his way.

10 All the ways of the LORD are loving and faithful
     toward those who keep the demands of his
       covenant.
11 For the sake of your name, LORD,
     forgive my iniquity, though it is great.

12 Who, then, are those who fear the LORD?
     He will instruct them in the ways they
       should choose.
13 They will spend their days in prosperity,
     and their descendants will inherit the land.
14 The LORD confides in those who fear him;
     he makes his covenant known to them.
15 My eyes are ever on the LORD,
     for only he will release my feet from the
       snare.

16 Turn to me and be gracious to me,
     for I am lonely and afflicted.
17 Relieve the troubles of my heart
     and free me from my anguish.
18 Look on my affliction and my distress
     and take away all my sins.
19 See how numerous are my enemies
     and how fiercely they hate me!

20 Guard my life and rescue me;
     do not let me be put to shame,
     for I take refuge in you.
21 May integrity and uprightness protect me,
     because my hope, LORD, is in you.

22 Deliver Israel, O God,
     from all their troubles!

PSALM 26

Of David.

1   Vindicate me, LORD,
     for I have led a blameless life;
   I have trusted in the LORD
     and have not faltered.
2   Test me, LORD, and try me,
     examine my heart and my mind;
3   for I have always been mindful of your
       unfailing love
   and have lived in reliance on your
     faithfulness.

4   I do not sit with the deceitful,
     nor do I associate with hypocrites.
5   I abhor the assembly of evildoers
     and refuse to sit with the wicked.
6   I wash my hands in innocence,
     and go about your altar, LORD,
7   proclaiming aloud your praise
     and telling of all your wonderful deeds.

8   LORD, I love the house where you live,
     the place where your glory dwells.
9   Do not take away my soul along with
       sinners,
   my life with those who are bloodthirsty,
10   in whose hands are wicked schemes,
     whose right hands are full of bribes.

11   I lead a blameless life;
         deliver me and be merciful to me.

12   My feet stand on level ground;
         in the great congregation I will praise the
            LORD.

PSALM 27

Of David.

1   The LORD is my light and my salvation —
        whom shall I fear?
    The LORD is the stronghold of my life —
        of whom shall I be afraid?

2   When the wicked advance against me
        to devour me,
    it is my enemies and my foes
        who will stumble and fall.
3   Though an army besiege me,
        my heart will not fear;
    though war break out against me,
        even then I will be confident.

4   One thing I ask from the LORD,
        this only do I seek:
    that I may dwell in the house of the LORD
        all the days of my life,
    to gaze on the beauty of the LORD
        and to seek him in his temple.
5   For in the day of trouble
        he will keep me safe in his dwelling;
    he will hide me in the shelter of his sacred tent
        and set me high upon a rock.

6   Then my head will be exalted
        above the enemies who surround me;

at his sacred tent I will sacrifice with shouts
of joy;
I will sing and make music to the LORD.

7   Hear my voice when I call, LORD;
be merciful to me and answer me.
8   My heart says of you, "Seek his face!"
Your face, LORD, I will seek.
9   Do not hide your face from me,
do not turn your servant away in anger;
you have been my helper.
Do not reject me or forsake me,
God my Savior.
10 Though my father and mother forsake me,
the LORD will receive me.
11 Teach me your way, LORD;
lead me in a straight path
because of my oppressors.
12 Do not turn me over to the desire of my
foes,
for false witnesses rise up against me,
spouting malicious accusations.

13 I remain confident of this:
I will see the goodness of the LORD
in the land of the living.
14 Wait for the LORD;
be strong and take heart
and wait for the LORD.

PSALM 28

Of David.

1   To you, Lord, I call;
    you are my Rock,
      do not turn a deaf ear to me.
  For if you remain silent,
    I will be like those who go down to the pit.

2   Hear my cry for mercy
    as I call to you for help,
  as I lift up my hands
    toward your Most Holy Place.

3   Do not drag me away with the wicked,
    with those who do evil,
  who speak cordially with their neighbors
    but harbor malice in their hearts.

4   Repay them for their deeds
    and for their evil work;
  repay them for what their hands have done
    and bring back on them what they deserve.

5   Because they have no regard for the deeds of
      the Lord
    and what his hands have done,
  he will tear them down
    and never build them up again.

6   Praise be to the Lord,
    for he has heard my cry for mercy.

7   The LORD is my strength and my shield;
        my heart trusts in him, and he helps me.
    My heart leaps for joy,
        and with my song I praise him.

8   The LORD is the strength of his people,
        a fortress of salvation for his anointed one.
9   Save your people and bless your inheritance;
        be their shepherd and carry them forever.

PSALM 29

A psalm of David.

1   Ascribe to the LORD, you heavenly beings,
        ascribe to the LORD glory and
            strength.
2   Ascribe to the LORD the glory due his
            name;
        worship the LORD in the splendor of
            his holiness.

3   The voice of the LORD is over the waters;
        the God of glory thunders,
        the LORD thunders over the mighty
            waters.
4   The voice of the LORD is powerful;
        the voice of the LORD is majestic.
5   The voice of the LORD breaks the cedars;
        the LORD breaks in pieces the cedars
            of Lebanon.
6   He makes Lebanon leap like a calf,
        Sirion like a young wild ox.
7   The voice of the LORD strikes
        with flashes of lightning.
8   The voice of the LORD shakes the desert;
        the LORD shakes the Desert of Kadesh.
9   The voice of the LORD twists the oaks
        and strips the forests bare.
    And in his temple all cry, "Glory!"

10   The LORD sits enthroned over the flood;
        the LORD is enthroned as King forever.
11   The LORD gives strength to his people;
        the LORD blesses his people with peace.

PSALM 30

A psalm. A song. For the dedication
of the temple. Of David.

1   I will exalt you, LORD,
      for you lifted me out of the depths
      and did not let my enemies gloat over me.

2   LORD my God, I called to you for help,
      and you healed me.

3   You, LORD, brought me up from the realm of
        the dead;
      you spared me from going down to the pit.

4   Sing the praises of the LORD, you his faithful
        people;
      praise his holy name.

5   For his anger lasts only a moment,
      but his favor lasts a lifetime;
    weeping may stay for the night,
      but rejoicing comes in the morning.

6   When I felt secure, I said,
      "I will never be shaken."

7   LORD, when you favored me,
      you made my royal mountain stand firm;
    but when you hid your face,
      I was dismayed.

8   To you, LORD, I called;
      to the Lord I cried for mercy:

9   "What is gained if I am silenced,
       if I go down to the pit?
    Will the dust praise you?
       Will it proclaim your faithfulness?
10   Hear, LORD, and be merciful to me;
       LORD, be my help."

11   You turned my wailing into dancing;
       you removed my sackcloth and clothed me
          with joy,
12   that my heart may sing your praises and not be
          silent.
    LORD my God, I will praise you forever.

PSALM 31

For the director of music. A psalm of David.

1 In you, LORD, I have taken refuge;
    let me never be put to shame;
    deliver me in your righteousness.
2 Turn your ear to me,
    come quickly to my rescue;
  be my rock of refuge,
    a strong fortress to save me.
3 Since you are my rock and my fortress,
    for the sake of your name lead and
        guide me.
4 Keep me free from the trap that is set for me,
    for you are my refuge.
5 Into your hands I commit my spirit;
    deliver me, LORD, my faithful God.

6 I hate those who cling to worthless idols;
    as for me, I trust in the LORD.
7 I will be glad and rejoice in your love,
    for you saw my affliction
    and knew the anguish of my soul.
8 You have not given me into the hands of the
        enemy
    but have set my feet in a spacious place.

9 Be merciful to me, LORD, for I am in distress;
    my eyes grow weak with sorrow,
    my soul and body with grief.

10 My life is consumed by anguish
and my years by groaning;
my strength fails because of my affliction,
and my bones grow weak.

11 Because of all my enemies,
I am the utter contempt of my neighbors
and an object of dread to my closest
friends —
those who see me on the street flee
from me.

12 I am forgotten as though I were dead;
I have become like broken pottery.

13 For I hear many whispering,
"Terror on every side!"
They conspire against me
and plot to take my life.

14 But I trust in you, LORD;
I say, "You are my God."

15 My times are in your hands;
deliver me from the hands of my
enemies,
from those who pursue me.

16 Let your face shine on your servant;
save me in your unfailing love.

17 Let me not be put to shame, LORD,
for I have cried out to you;
but let the wicked be put to shame
and be silent in the realm of the dead.

18 Let their lying lips be silenced,
for with pride and contempt
they speak arrogantly against the righteous.

19   How abundant are the good things
              that you have stored up for those who fear
                    you,
          that you bestow in the sight of all,
              on those who take refuge in you.
20   In the shelter of your presence you hide them
              from all human intrigues;
          you keep them safe in your dwelling
              from accusing tongues.

21   Praise be to the Lord,
              for he showed me the wonders of his love
              when I was in a city under siege.
22   In my alarm I said,
              "I am cut off from your sight!"
          Yet you heard my cry for mercy
              when I called to you for help.

23   Love the Lord, all his faithful people!
              The Lord preserves those who are true to
                    him,
          but the proud he pays back in full.
24   Be strong and take heart,
              all you who hope in the Lord.

PSALM 32

Of David. A maskil.

1 Blessed is the one
   whose transgressions are forgiven,
   whose sins are covered.

2 Blessed is the one
   whose sin the LORD does not count against
      them
   and in whose spirit is no deceit.

3 When I kept silent,
   my bones wasted away
   through my groaning all day long.

4 For day and night
   your hand was heavy on me;
my strength was sapped
   as in the heat of summer.

5 Then I acknowledged my sin to you
   and did not cover up my iniquity.
I said, "I will confess
   my transgressions to the LORD."
And you forgave
   the guilt of my sin.

6 Therefore let all the faithful pray to you
   while you may be found;
surely the rising of the mighty waters
   will not reach them.

7   You are my hiding place;
        you will protect me from trouble
        and surround me with songs of deliverance.

8   I will instruct you and teach you in the way
            you should go;
        I will counsel you with my loving eye on
            you.
9   Do not be like the horse or the mule,
        which have no understanding
    but must be controlled by bit and bridle
        or they will not come to you.
10   Many are the woes of the wicked,
        but the LORD's unfailing love
        surrounds the one who trusts in him.

11   Rejoice in the LORD and be glad, you
            righteous;
        sing, all you who are upright in heart!

PSALM 33

1 Sing joyfully to the LORD, you righteous;
      it is fitting for the upright to praise him.
2 Praise the LORD with the harp;
      make music to him on the ten-stringed lyre.
3 Sing to him a new song;
      play skillfully, and shout for joy.

4 For the word of the LORD is right and true;
      he is faithful in all he does.
5 The LORD loves righteousness and justice;
      the earth is full of his unfailing love.

6 By the word of the LORD the heavens were
        made,
      their starry host by the breath of his
        mouth.
7 He gathers the waters of the sea into jars;
      he puts the deep into storehouses.
8 Let all the earth fear the LORD;
      let all the people of the world revere him.
9 For he spoke, and it came to be;
      he commanded, and it stood firm.

10 The LORD foils the plans of the nations;
       he thwarts the purposes of the peoples.
11 But the plans of the LORD stand firm forever,
       the purposes of his heart through all
         generations.

12 Blessed is the nation whose God is the LORD,
    the people he chose for his inheritance.
13 From heaven the LORD looks down
    and sees all mankind;
14 from his dwelling place he watches
    all who live on earth —
15 he who forms the hearts of all,
    who considers everything they do.

16 No king is saved by the size of his army;
    no warrior escapes by his great strength.
17 A horse is a vain hope for deliverance;
    despite all its great strength it cannot save.
18 But the eyes of the LORD are on those who
    fear him,
    on those whose hope is in his unfailing
    love,
19 to deliver them from death
    and keep them alive in famine.

20 We wait in hope for the LORD;
    he is our help and our shield.
21 In him our hearts rejoice,
    for we trust in his holy name.
22 May your unfailing love be with us, LORD,
    even as we put our hope in you.

PSALM 34

*Of David. When he pretended to be insane before
Abimelek, who drove him away, and he left.*

1 I will extol the LORD at all times;
    his praise will always be on my lips.
2 I will glory in the LORD;
    let the afflicted hear and rejoice.
3 Glorify the LORD with me;
    let us exalt his name together.

4 I sought the LORD, and he answered me;
    he delivered me from all my fears.
5 Those who look to him are radiant;
    their faces are never covered with shame.
6 This poor man called, and the LORD heard him;
    he saved him out of all his troubles.
7 The angel of the LORD encamps around those
        who fear him,
    and he delivers them.

8 Taste and see that the LORD is good;
    blessed is the one who takes refuge in him.
9 Fear the LORD, you his holy people,
    for those who fear him lack nothing.
10 The lions may grow weak and hungry,
    but those who seek the LORD lack no good
        thing.
11 Come, my children, listen to me;
    I will teach you the fear of the LORD.

12 Whoever of you loves life
and desires to see many good days,
13 keep your tongue from evil
and your lips from telling lies.
14 Turn from evil and do good;
seek peace and pursue it.

15 The eyes of the Lord are on the righteous,
and his ears are attentive to their cry;
16 but the face of the Lord is against those who
do evil,
to blot out their name from the earth.

17 The righteous cry out, and the Lord hears
them;
he delivers them from all their troubles.
18 The Lord is close to the brokenhearted
and saves those who are crushed in spirit.

19 The righteous person may have many troubles,
but the Lord delivers him from them all;
20 he protects all his bones,
not one of them will be broken.

21 Evil will slay the wicked;
the foes of the righteous will be condemned.
22 The Lord will rescue his servants;
no one who takes refuge in him will be
condemned.

PSALM 35

Of David.

1 Contend, LORD, with those who contend
      with me;
  fight against those who fight against me.
2 Take up shield and armor;
  arise and come to my aid.
3 Brandish spear and javelin
  against those who pursue me.
Say to me,
  "I am your salvation."

4 May those who seek my life
  be disgraced and put to shame;
may those who plot my ruin
  be turned back in dismay.
5 May they be like chaff before the wind,
  with the angel of the LORD driving them
      away;
6 may their path be dark and slippery,
  with the angel of the LORD pursuing them.

7 Since they hid their net for me without cause
  and without cause dug a pit for me,
8 may ruin overtake them by surprise —
  may the net they hid entangle them,
  may they fall into the pit, to their ruin.
9 Then my soul will rejoice in the LORD
  and delight in his salvation.

10　My whole being will exclaim,
　　　"Who is like you, LORD?
　　You rescue the poor from those too strong
　　　　　for them,
　　　　the poor and needy from those who rob
　　　　　them."

11　Ruthless witnesses come forward;
　　　they question me on things I know
　　　　　nothing about.
12　They repay me evil for good
　　　and leave me like one bereaved.
13　Yet when they were ill, I put on sackcloth
　　　and humbled myself with fasting.
　　When my prayers returned to me
　　　　unanswered,
14　　I went about mourning
　　　as though for my friend or brother.
　　I bowed my head in grief
　　　as though weeping for my mother.
15　But when I stumbled, they gathered in glee;
　　　assailants gathered against me without
　　　　　my knowledge.
　　They slandered me without ceasing.
16　Like the ungodly they maliciously mocked;
　　　they gnashed their teeth at me.

17　How long, Lord, will you look on?
　　　Rescue me from their ravages,
　　　my precious life from these lions.
18　I will give you thanks in the great assembly;
　　　among the throngs I will praise you.

19   Do not let those gloat over me
        who are my enemies without cause;
     do not let those who hate me without reason
        maliciously wink the eye.
20   They do not speak peaceably,
        but devise false accusations
        against those who live quietly in the land.
21   They sneer at me and say, "Aha! Aha!
        With our own eyes we have seen it."

22   LORD, you have seen this; do not be silent.
        Do not be far from me, Lord.
23   Awake, and rise to my defense!
        Contend for me, my God and Lord.
24   Vindicate me in your righteousness, LORD
              my God;
        do not let them gloat over me.
25   Do not let them think, "Aha, just what we
              wanted!"
        or say, "We have swallowed him up."

26   May all who gloat over my distress
        be put to shame and confusion;
     may all who exalt themselves over me
        be clothed with shame and disgrace.
27   May those who delight in my vindication
        shout for joy and gladness;
     may they always say, "The LORD be exalted,
        who delights in the well-being of his
              servant."

28   My tongue will proclaim your righteousness,
        your praises all day long.

PSALM 36

For the director of music. Of David the servant of the LORD.

1   I have a message from God in my heart
        concerning the sinfulness of the wicked:
    There is no fear of God
        before their eyes.

2   In their own eyes they flatter themselves
        too much to detect or hate their sin.

3   The words of their mouths are wicked and
            deceitful;
        they fail to act wisely or do good.

4   Even on their beds they plot evil;
        they commit themselves to a sinful course
        and do not reject what is wrong.

5   Your love, LORD, reaches to the heavens,
        your faithfulness to the skies.

6   Your righteousness is like the highest
            mountains,
        your justice like the great deep.
    You, LORD, preserve both people and
            animals.

7   How priceless is your unfailing love, O God!
        People take refuge in the shadow of your
            wings.

8   They feast on the abundance of your house;
        you give them drink from your river of
            delights.

9   For with you is the fountain of life;
          in your light we see light.

10   Continue your love to those who know you,
          your righteousness to the upright in heart.

11   May the foot of the proud not come
             against me,
          nor the hand of the wicked drive me away.

12   See how the evildoers lie fallen —
          thrown down, not able to rise!

PSALM 37

Of David.

1   Do not fret because of those who are evil
     or be envious of those who do wrong;
2   for like the grass they will soon wither,
     like green plants they will soon die away.

3   Trust in the Lord and do good;
     dwell in the land and enjoy safe pasture.
4   Take delight in the Lord,
     and he will give you the desires of your
         heart.

5   Commit your way to the Lord;
     trust in him and he will do this:
6   He will make your righteous reward shine
         like the dawn,
     your vindication like the noonday sun.

7   Be still before the Lord
     and wait patiently for him;
   do not fret when people succeed in their ways,
     when they carry out their wicked
         schemes.

8   Refrain from anger and turn from wrath;
     do not fret — it leads only to evil.
9   For those who are evil will be destroyed,
     but those who hope in the Lord will inherit
         the land.

10   A little while, and the wicked will be no more;
         though you look for them, they will not be
             found.
11   But the meek will inherit the land
         and enjoy peace and prosperity.

12   The wicked plot against the righteous
         and gnash their teeth at them;
13   but the Lord laughs at the wicked,
         for he knows their day is coming.

14   The wicked draw the sword
         and bend the bow
     to bring down the poor and needy,
         to slay those whose ways are upright.
15   But their swords will pierce their own hearts,
         and their bows will be broken.

16   Better the little that the righteous have
         than the wealth of many wicked;
17   for the power of the wicked will be broken,
         but the LORD upholds the righteous.

18   The blameless spend their days under the
             LORD's care,
         and their inheritance will endure forever.
19   In times of disaster they will not wither;
         in days of famine they will enjoy plenty.

20   But the wicked will perish:
         Though the LORD's enemies are like the
             flowers of the field,
         they will be consumed, they will go up in
             smoke.

21   The wicked borrow and do not repay,
        but the righteous give generously;
22   those the LORD blesses will inherit the land,
        but those he curses will be destroyed.

23   The LORD makes firm the steps
        of the one who delights in him;
24   though he may stumble, he will not fall,
        for the LORD upholds him with his hand.

25   I was young and now I am old,
        yet I have never seen the righteous
            forsaken
        or their children begging bread.
26   They are always generous and lend freely;
        their children will be a blessing.

27   Turn from evil and do good;
        then you will dwell in the land forever.
28   For the LORD loves the just
        and will not forsake his faithful ones.

        Wrongdoers will be completely destroyed;
        the offspring of the wicked will perish.
29   The righteous will inherit the land
        and dwell in it forever.

30   The mouths of the righteous utter wisdom,
        and their tongues speak what is just.
31   The law of their God is in their hearts;
        their feet do not slip.

32   The wicked lie in wait for the righteous,
        intent on putting them to death;

33 but the LORD will not leave them in the power
of the wicked
or let them be condemned when brought
to trial.

34 Hope in the LORD
and keep his way.
He will exalt you to inherit the land;
when the wicked are destroyed, you will
see it.

35 I have seen a wicked and ruthless man
flourishing like a luxuriant native tree,
36 but he soon passed away and was no more;
though I looked for him, he could not be
found.

37 Consider the blameless, observe the upright;
a future awaits those who seek peace.
38 But all sinners will be destroyed;
there will be no future for the wicked.

39 The salvation of the righteous comes from the
LORD;
he is their stronghold in time of trouble.
40 The LORD helps them and delivers them;
he delivers them from the wicked and saves
them,
because they take refuge in him.

PSALM 38

A psalm of David. A petition.

1   L ord, do not rebuke me in your anger
    or discipline me in your wrath.
2   Your arrows have pierced me,
    and your hand has come down on me.
3   Because of your wrath there is no health in my
        body;
    there is no soundness in my bones because
        of my sin.
4   My guilt has overwhelmed me
    like a burden too heavy to bear.

5   My wounds fester and are loathsome
    because of my sinful folly.
6   I am bowed down and brought very low;
    all day long I go about mourning.
7   My back is filled with searing pain;
    there is no health in my body.
8   I am feeble and utterly crushed;
    I groan in anguish of heart.

9   All my longings lie open before you, Lord;
    my sighing is not hidden from you.
10 My heart pounds, my strength fails me;
    even the light has gone from my eyes.
11 My friends and companions avoid me because
    of my wounds;
    my neighbors stay far away.

12   Those who want to kill me set their traps,
         those who would harm me talk of my ruin;
         all day long they scheme and lie.

13   I am like the deaf, who cannot hear,
         like the mute, who cannot speak;
14   I have become like one who does not hear,
         whose mouth can offer no reply.
15   LORD, I wait for you;
         you will answer, Lord my God.
16   For I said, "Do not let them gloat
         or exalt themselves over me when my feet
            slip."

17   For I am about to fall,
         and my pain is ever with me.
18   I confess my iniquity;
         I am troubled by my sin.
19   Many have become my enemies without cause;
         those who hate me without reason are
            numerous.
20   Those who repay my good with evil
         lodge accusations against me,
         though I seek only to do what is good.

21   LORD, do not forsake me;
         do not be far from me, my God.
22   Come quickly to help me,
         my Lord and my Savior.

PSALM 39

For the director of music. For Jeduthun.
A psalm of David.

1 I said, "I will watch my ways
    and keep my tongue from sin;
  I will put a muzzle on my mouth
    while in the presence of the wicked."

2 So I remained utterly silent,
    not even saying anything good.
  But my anguish increased;
3   my heart grew hot within me.
  While I meditated, the fire burned;
    then I spoke with my tongue:

4 "Show me, Lord, my life's end
    and the number of my days;
    let me know how fleeting my life is.
5 You have made my days a mere handbreadth;
    the span of my years is as nothing before
      you.
  Everyone is but a breath,
    even those who seem secure.

6 "Surely everyone goes around like a mere
      phantom;
    in vain they rush about, heaping up wealth
    without knowing whose it will finally be.

7 "But now, Lord, what do I look for?
    My hope is in you.

8   Save me from all my transgressions;
         do not make me the scorn of fools.
9   I was silent; I would not open my mouth,
         for you are the one who has done this.
10   Remove your scourge from me;
         I am overcome by the blow of your hand.
11   When you rebuke and discipline anyone for
             their sin,
         you consume their wealth like a moth —
         surely everyone is but a breath.

12   "Hear my prayer, LORD,
         listen to my cry for help;
         do not be deaf to my weeping.
     I dwell with you as a foreigner,
         a stranger, as all my ancestors were.
13   Look away from me, that I may enjoy life again
         before I depart and am no more."

PSALM 40

For the director of music. Of David. A psalm.

1 I waited patiently for the LORD;
     he turned to me and heard my cry.
2 He lifted me out of the slimy pit,
     out of the mud and mire;
   he set my feet on a rock
     and gave me a firm place to stand.
3 He put a new song in my mouth,
     a hymn of praise to our God.
   Many will see and fear the LORD
     and put their trust in him.

4 Blessed is the one
     who trusts in the LORD,
   who does not look to the proud,
     to those who turn aside to false gods.
5 Many, LORD my God,
     are the wonders you have done,
     the things you planned for us.
   None can compare with you;
     were I to speak and tell of your deeds,
     they would be too many to declare.

6 Sacrifice and offering you did not
          desire —
     but my ears you have opened —
     burnt offerings and sin offerings you
          did not require.

7 Then I said, "Here I am, I have come —
  it is written about me in the scroll.
8 I desire to do your will, my God;
  your law is within my heart."

9 I proclaim your saving acts in the great
   assembly;
  I do not seal my lips, Lord,
  as you know.
10 I do not hide your righteousness in my heart;
  I speak of your faithfulness and your saving
   help.
  I do not conceal your love and your
   faithfulness
  from the great assembly.

11 Do not withhold your mercy from me, Lord;
  may your love and faithfulness always
   protect me.
12 For troubles without number surround me;
  my sins have overtaken me, and I cannot
   see.
  They are more than the hairs of my head,
  and my heart fails within me.
13 Be pleased to save me, Lord;
  come quickly, Lord, to help me.

14 May all who want to take my life
  be put to shame and confusion;
 may all who desire my ruin
  be turned back in disgrace.
15 May those who say to me, "Aha! Aha!"
  be appalled at their own shame.

16 But may all who seek you
        rejoice and be glad in you;
    may those who long for your saving help
            always say,
        "The LORD is great!"

17 But as for me, I am poor and needy;
        may the Lord think of me.
    You are my help and my deliverer;
        you are my God, do not delay.

PSALM 41

For the director of music. A psalm of David.

1   Blessed are those who have regard for the
        weak;
        the LORD delivers them in times of
        trouble.
2   The LORD protects and preserves them —
        they are counted among the blessed in
        the land —
        he does not give them over to the desire
        of their foes.
3   The LORD sustains them on their sickbed
        and restores them from their bed of
        illness.

4   I said, "Have mercy on me, LORD;
        heal me, for I have sinned against you."
5   My enemies say of me in malice,
        "When will he die and his name perish?"
6   When one of them comes to see me,
        he speaks falsely, while his heart gathers
        slander;
        then he goes out and spreads it around.

7   All my enemies whisper together against me;
        they imagine the worst for me, saying,
8   "A vile disease has afflicted him;
        he will never get up from the place where
        he lies."

9   Even my close friend,
          someone I trusted,
    one who shared my bread,
          has turned against me.

10   But may you have mercy on me, LORD;
          raise me up, that I may repay them.
11   I know that you are pleased with me,
          for my enemy does not triumph over me.
12   Because of my integrity you uphold me
          and set me in your presence forever.

13   Praise be to the LORD, the God of Israel,
          from everlasting to everlasting.
                Amen and Amen.

BOOK II

Psalms 42 – 72

PSALM 42

*For the director of music. A maskil
of the Sons of Korah.*

1   As the deer pants for streams of water,
     so my soul pants for you, my God.
2   My soul thirsts for God, for the living God.
     When can I go and meet with God?
3   My tears have been my food
     day and night,
   while people say to me all day long,
     "Where is your God?"
4   These things I remember
     as I pour out my soul:
   how I used to go to the house of God
     under the protection of the Mighty One
   with shouts of joy and praise
     among the festive throng.

5   Why, my soul, are you downcast?
     Why so disturbed within me?
   Put your hope in God,
     for I will yet praise him,
     my Savior and my God.

6   My soul is downcast within me;
     therefore I will remember you
   from the land of the Jordan,
     the heights of Hermon — from Mount
       Mizar.

7   Deep calls to deep
          in the roar of your waterfalls;
      all your waves and breakers
          have swept over me.

8   By day the LORD directs his love,
          at night his song is with me —
      a prayer to the God of my life.

9   I say to God my Rock,
          "Why have you forgotten me?
      Why must I go about mourning,
          oppressed by the enemy?"

10   My bones suffer mortal agony
          as my foes taunt me,
      saying to me all day long,
          "Where is your God?"

11   Why, my soul, are you downcast?
          Why so disturbed within me?
      Put your hope in God,
          for I will yet praise him,
          my Savior and my God.

PSALM 43

1 Vindicate me, my God,
   and plead my cause
   against an unfaithful nation.
Rescue me from those who are
   deceitful and wicked.

2 You are God my stronghold.
   Why have you rejected me?
Why must I go about mourning,
   oppressed by the enemy?

3 Send me your light and your faithful care,
   let them lead me;
let them bring me to your holy mountain,
   to the place where you dwell.

4 Then I will go to the altar of God,
   to God, my joy and my delight.
I will praise you with the lyre,
   O God, my God.

5 Why, my soul, are you downcast?
   Why so disturbed within me?
Put your hope in God,
   for I will yet praise him,
   my Savior and my God.

PSALM 44

For the director of music. Of the Sons of Korah. A maskil.

1 We have heard it with our ears, O God;
   our ancestors have told us
what you did in their days,
   in days long ago.

2 With your hand you drove out the nations
   and planted our ancestors;
you crushed the peoples
   and made our ancestors flourish.

3 It was not by their sword that they won the
      land,
   nor did their arm bring them victory;
it was your right hand, your arm,
   and the light of your face, for you loved
      them.

4 You are my King and my God,
   who decrees victories for Jacob.

5 Through you we push back our enemies;
   through your name we trample our foes.

6 I put no trust in my bow,
   my sword does not bring me victory;

7 but you give us victory over our enemies,
   you put our adversaries to shame.

8 In God we make our boast all day long,
   and we will praise your name forever.

9   But now you have rejected and humbled us;
         you no longer go out with our armies.
10   You made us retreat before the enemy,
         and our adversaries have plundered us.
11   You gave us up to be devoured like sheep
         and have scattered us among the nations.
12   You sold your people for a pittance,
         gaining nothing from their sale.

13   You have made us a reproach to our
             neighbors,
         the scorn and derision of those around us.
14   You have made us a byword among the
             nations;
         the peoples shake their heads at us.
15   I live in disgrace all day long,
         and my face is covered with shame
16   at the taunts of those who reproach and
             revile me,
         because of the enemy, who is bent on
             revenge.

17   All this came upon us,
         though we had not forgotten you;
         we had not been false to your covenant.
18   Our hearts had not turned back;
         our feet had not strayed from your path.
19   But you crushed us and made us a haunt for
             jackals;
         you covered us over with deep darkness.

20   If we had forgotten the name of our God
         or spread out our hands to a foreign god,

21   would not God have discovered it,
         since he knows the secrets of the heart?
22   Yet for your sake we face death all day long;
         we are considered as sheep to be
             slaughtered.

23   Awake, Lord! Why do you sleep?
         Rouse yourself! Do not reject us forever.
24   Why do you hide your face
         and forget our misery and oppression?

25   We are brought down to the dust;
         our bodies cling to the ground.
26   Rise up and help us;
         rescue us because of your unfailing love.

PSALM 45

For the director of music. To the tune of "Lilies."
Of the Sons of Korah. A maskil.
A wedding song.

1   My heart is stirred by a noble theme
        as I recite my verses for the king;
        my tongue is the pen of a skillful writer.

2   You are the most excellent of men
        and your lips have been anointed with
            grace,
        since God has blessed you forever.

3   Gird your sword on your side, you mighty one;
        clothe yourself with splendor and majesty.

4   In your majesty ride forth victoriously
        in the cause of truth, humility and justice;
        let your right hand achieve awesome deeds.

5   Let your sharp arrows pierce the hearts of the
            king's enemies;
        let the nations fall beneath your feet.

6   Your throne, O God, will last for ever and
            ever;
        a scepter of justice will be the scepter of
            your kingdom.

7   You love righteousness and hate wickedness;
        therefore God, your God, has set you above
            your companions
        by anointing you with the oil of joy.

8   All your robes are fragrant with myrrh and
            aloes and cassia;
        from palaces adorned with ivory
        the music of the strings makes you glad.
9   Daughters of kings are among your honored
            women;
        at your right hand is the royal bride in gold
            of Ophir.

10 Listen, daughter, and pay careful attention:
        Forget your people and your father's house.
11 Let the king be enthralled by your beauty;
        honor him, for he is your lord.
12 The city of Tyre will come with a gift,
        people of wealth will seek your favor.
13 All glorious is the princess within her chamber;
        her gown is interwoven with gold.
14 In embroidered garments she is led to the
            king;
        her virgin companions follow her —
        those brought to be with her.
15 Led in with joy and gladness,
        they enter the palace of the king.

16 Your sons will take the place of your fathers;
        you will make them princes throughout the
            land.

17 I will perpetuate your memory through all
            generations;
        therefore the nations will praise you for ever
            and ever.

PSALM 46

For the director of music. Of the Sons of Korah. According to alamoth. *A song.*

1 God is our refuge and strength,
an ever-present help in trouble.

2 Therefore we will not fear, though the earth
give way
and the mountains fall into the heart of the
sea,

3 though its waters roar and foam
and the mountains quake with their surging.

4 There is a river whose streams make glad the
city of God,
the holy place where the Most High dwells.

5 God is within her, she will not fall;
God will help her at break of day.

6 Nations are in uproar, kingdoms fall;
he lifts his voice, the earth melts.

7 The LORD Almighty is with us;
the God of Jacob is our fortress.

8 Come and see what the LORD has done,
the desolations he has brought on the earth.

9 He makes wars cease
to the ends of the earth.
He breaks the bow and shatters the spear;
he burns the shields with fire.

10   He says, "Be still, and know that I am God;
        I will be exalted among the nations,
        I will be exalted in the earth."

11   The Lord Almighty is with us;
        the God of Jacob is our fortress.

PSALM 47

For the director of music. Of the Sons of Korah. A psalm.

1 Clap your hands, all you nations;
  shout to God with cries of joy.

2 For the Lord Most High is awesome,
  the great King over all the earth.
3 He subdued nations under us,
  peoples under our feet.
4 He chose our inheritance for us,
  the pride of Jacob, whom he loved.

5 God has ascended amid shouts of joy,
  the Lord amid the sounding of trumpets.
6 Sing praises to God, sing praises;
  sing praises to our King, sing praises.
7 For God is the King of all the earth;
  sing to him a psalm of praise.

8 God reigns over the nations;
  God is seated on his holy throne.
9 The nobles of the nations assemble
  as the people of the God of Abraham,
for the kings of the earth belong to God;
  he is greatly exalted.

PSALM 48

A song. A psalm of the Sons of Korah.

1   Great is the Lord, and most worthy of praise,
      in the city of our God, his holy mountain.

2   Beautiful in its loftiness,
      the joy of the whole earth,
   like the heights of Zaphon is Mount Zion,
      the city of the Great King.
3   God is in her citadels;
      he has shown himself to be her fortress.

4   When the kings joined forces,
      when they advanced together,
5   they saw her and were astounded;
      they fled in terror.
6   Trembling seized them there,
      pain like that of a woman in labor.
7   You destroyed them like ships of Tarshish
      shattered by an east wind.

8   As we have heard,
      so we have seen
   in the city of the Lord Almighty,
      in the city of our God:
   God makes her secure
      forever.

9   Within your temple, O God,
      we meditate on your unfailing love.

10 Like your name, O God,
   your praise reaches to the ends of the earth;
   your right hand is filled with righteousness.
11 Mount Zion rejoices,
   the villages of Judah are glad
   because of your judgments.

12 Walk about Zion, go around her,
   count her towers,
13 consider well her ramparts,
   view her citadels,
   that you may tell of them
   to the next generation.

14 For this God is our God for ever and ever;
   he will be our guide even to the end.

PSALM 49

For the director of music. Of the Sons of Korah. A psalm.

1 Hear this, all you peoples;
  listen, all who live in this world,
2 both low and high,
  rich and poor alike:
3 My mouth will speak words of wisdom;
  the meditation of my heart will give you
    understanding.
4 I will turn my ear to a proverb;
  with the harp I will expound my riddle:

5 Why should I fear when evil days come,
  when wicked deceivers surround me —
6 those who trust in their wealth
  and boast of their great riches?
7 No one can redeem the life of another
  or give to God a ransom for them —
8 the ransom for a life is costly,
  no payment is ever enough —
9 so that they should live on forever
  and not see decay.
10 For all can see that the wise die,
  that the foolish and the senseless also perish,
    leaving their wealth to others.
11 Their tombs will remain their houses forever,
  their dwellings for endless generations,
  though they had named lands after
    themselves.

12　People, despite their wealth, do not endure;
　　　　they are like the beasts that perish.

13　This is the fate of those who trust in themselves,
　　　　and of their followers, who approve their
　　　　　　sayings.
14　They are like sheep and are destined to die;
　　　　death will be their shepherd
　　　　(but the upright will prevail over them in
　　　　　　the morning).
　　Their forms will decay in the grave,
　　　　far from their princely mansions.
15　But God will redeem me from the realm of the
　　　　dead;
　　　　he will surely take me to himself.
16　Do not be overawed when others grow rich,
　　　　when the splendor of their houses increases;
17　for they will take nothing with them when they
　　　　die,
　　　　their splendor will not descend with them.
18　Though while they live they count themselves
　　　　blessed —
　　　　and people praise you when you prosper —
19　they will join those who have gone before
　　　　them,
　　　　who will never again see the light of life.

20　People who have wealth but lack
　　　　understanding
　　　　are like the beasts that perish.

PSALM 50

A psalm of Asaph.

1 The Mighty One, God, the LORD,
    speaks and summons the earth
    from the rising of the sun to where it
        sets.
2 From Zion, perfect in beauty,
    God shines forth.
3 Our God comes
    and will not be silent;
a fire devours before him,
    and around him a tempest rages.
4 He summons the heavens above,
    and the earth, that he may judge his
        people:
5 "Gather to me this consecrated people,
    who made a covenant with me by
        sacrifice."
6 And the heavens proclaim his righteousness,
    for he is a God of justice.

7 "Listen, my people, and I will speak;
    I will testify against you, Israel:
    I am God, your God.
8 I bring no charges against you concerning
        your sacrifices
    or concerning your burnt offerings, which
        are ever before me.

9   I have no need of a bull from your stall
         or of goats from your pens,
10   for every animal of the forest is mine,
         and the cattle on a thousand hills.
11   I know every bird in the mountains,
         and the insects in the fields are mine.
12   If I were hungry I would not tell you,
         for the world is mine, and all that is in it.
13   Do I eat the flesh of bulls
         or drink the blood of goats?

14   "Sacrifice thank offerings to God,
         fulfill your vows to the Most High,
15   and call on me in the day of trouble;
         I will deliver you, and you will honor me."

16 But to the wicked person, God says:

    "What right have you to recite my laws
         or take my covenant on your lips?
17   You hate my instruction
         and cast my words behind you.
18   When you see a thief, you join with him;
         you throw in your lot with adulterers.
19   You use your mouth for evil
         and harness your tongue to deceit.
20   You sit and testify against your brother
         and slander your own mother's son.
21   When you did these things and I kept silent,
         you thought I was exactly like you.
    But I now arraign you
         and set my accusations before you.

22   "Consider this, you who forget God,
          or I will tear you to pieces, with no one
             to rescue you:
23   Those who sacrifice thank offerings
             honor me,
          and to the blameless I will show my
             salvation."

PSALM 51

*For the director of music. A psalm of David. When
the prophet Nathan came to him after David
had committed adultery with Bathsheba.*

1 Have mercy on me, O God,
    according to your unfailing love;
according to your great compassion
    blot out my transgressions.
2 Wash away all my iniquity
    and cleanse me from my sin.

3 For I know my transgressions,
    and my sin is always before me.
4 Against you, you only, have I sinned
    and done what is evil in your sight;
so you are right in your verdict
    and justified when you judge.
5 Surely I was sinful at birth,
    sinful from the time my mother
        conceived me.
6 Yet you desired faithfulness even in the womb;
    you taught me wisdom in that secret place.

7 Cleanse me with hyssop, and I will be clean;
    wash me, and I will be whiter than snow.
8 Let me hear joy and gladness;
    let the bones you have crushed rejoice.
9 Hide your face from my sins
    and blot out all my iniquity.

10   Create in me a pure heart, O God,
        and renew a steadfast spirit within me.
11   Do not cast me from your presence
        or take your Holy Spirit from me.
12   Restore to me the joy of your salvation
        and grant me a willing spirit, to sustain me.

13   Then I will teach transgressors your ways,
        so that sinners will turn back to you.
14   Deliver me from the guilt of bloodshed, O God,
        you who are God my Savior,
        and my tongue will sing of your
           righteousness.
15   Open my lips, Lord,
        and my mouth will declare your praise.
16   You do not delight in sacrifice, or I would
           bring it;
        you do not take pleasure in burnt offerings.
17   My sacrifice, O God, is a broken spirit;
        a broken and contrite heart
        you, God, will not despise.

18   May it please you to prosper Zion,
        to build up the walls of Jerusalem.
19   Then you will delight in the sacrifices of the
           righteous,
        in burnt offerings offered whole;
        then bulls will be offered on your altar.

PSALM 52

For the director of music. A maskil *of David. When Doeg the Edomite had gone to Saul and told him: "David has gone to the house of Ahimelek."*

1   Why do you boast of evil, you mighty
        hero?
        Why do you boast all day long,
        you who are a disgrace in the eyes of
        God?

2   You who practice deceit,
        your tongue plots destruction;
        it is like a sharpened razor.

3   You love evil rather than good,
        falsehood rather than speaking the truth.

4   You love every harmful word,
        you deceitful tongue!

5   Surely God will bring you down to everlasting
        ruin:
        He will snatch you up and pluck you from
            your tent;
        he will uproot you from the land of the
            living.

6   The righteous will see and fear;
        they will laugh at you, saying,

7   "Here now is the man
        who did not make God his stronghold
    but trusted in his great wealth
        and grew strong by destroying others!"

8   But I am like an olive tree
         flourishing in the house of God;
     I trust in God's unfailing love
         for ever and ever.
9   For what you have done I will always praise
             you
         in the presence of your faithful people.
     And I will hope in your name,
         for your name is good.

PSALM 53

For the director of music. According to
mahalath. *A maskil of David.*

1   The fool says in his heart,
    "There is no God."
They are corrupt, and their ways are vile;
    there is no one who does good.

2   God looks down from heaven
    on all mankind
to see if there are any who understand,
    any who seek God.

3   Everyone has turned away, all have become
        corrupt;
    there is no one who does good,
    not even one.

4   Do all these evildoers know nothing?

They devour my people as though eating
        bread;
    they never call on God.

5   But there they are, overwhelmed with
        dread,
    where there was nothing to dread.
God scattered the bones of those who attacked
        you;
    you put them to shame, for God despised
        them.

6   Oh, that salvation for Israel would come out of
        Zion!
    When God restores his people,
    let Jacob rejoice and Israel be glad!

PSALM 54

*For the director of music. With stringed instruments.
A maskil of David. When the Ziphites had gone to
Saul and said, "Is not David hiding among us?"*

1 Save me, O God, by your name;
   vindicate me by your might.
2 Hear my prayer, O God;
   listen to the words of my mouth.

3 Arrogant foes are attacking me;
   ruthless people are trying to kill me —
   people without regard for God.

4 Surely God is my help;
   the Lord is the one who sustains me.

5 Let evil recoil on those who slander me;
   in your faithfulness destroy them.

6 I will sacrifice a freewill offering to you;
   I will praise your name, LORD, for it is good.
7 You have delivered me from all my troubles,
   and my eyes have looked in triumph on my
      foes.

PSALM 55

*For the director of music. With stringed
instruments. A maskil of David.*

1 Listen to my prayer, O God,
   do not ignore my plea;
2   hear me and answer me.
   My thoughts trouble me and I am distraught
3   because of what my enemy is saying,
      because of the threats of the wicked;
   for they bring down suffering on me
      and assail me in their anger.

4 My heart is in anguish within me;
      the terrors of death have fallen on me.
5 Fear and trembling have beset me;
      horror has overwhelmed me.
6 I said, "Oh, that I had the wings of a dove!
      I would fly away and be at rest.
7 I would flee far away
      and stay in the desert;
8 I would hurry to my place of shelter,
      far from the tempest and storm."

9 Lord, confuse the wicked, confound their
            words,
      for I see violence and strife in the city.
10 Day and night they prowl about on its
            walls;
      malice and abuse are within it.

11   Destructive forces are at work in the
                   city;
        threats and lies never leave its
               streets.

12   If an enemy were insulting me,
        I could endure it;
    if a foe were rising against me,
        I could hide.
13   But it is you, a man like myself,
        my companion, my close friend,
14   with whom I once enjoyed sweet fellowship
        at the house of God,
    as we walked about
        among the worshipers.

15   Let death take my enemies by surprise;
        let them go down alive to the realm
           of the dead,
        for evil finds lodging among them.

16   As for me, I call to God,
        and the Lord saves me.
17   Evening, morning and noon
        I cry out in distress,
        and he hears my voice.
18   He rescues me unharmed
        from the battle waged against me,
        even though many oppose me.
19   God, who is enthroned from of old,
        who does not change —
    he will hear them and humble them,
        because they have no fear of God.

20 My companion attacks his friends;
         he violates his covenant.
21 His talk is smooth as butter,
         yet war is in his heart;
    his words are more soothing than oil,
         yet they are drawn swords.

22 Cast your cares on the LORD
         and he will sustain you;
    he will never let
         the righteous be shaken.
23 But you, God, will bring down the wicked
         into the pit of decay;
    the bloodthirsty and deceitful
         will not live out half their days.

    But as for me, I trust in you.

PSALM 56

*For the director of music. To the tune of "A Dove
on Distant Oaks." Of David. A* miktam. *When
the Philistines had seized him in Gath.*

1 Be merciful to me, my God,
for my enemies are in hot pursuit;
all day long they press their attack.
2 My adversaries pursue me all day long;
in their pride many are attacking me.

3 When I am afraid, I put my trust in you.
4 In God, whose word I praise —
in God I trust and am not afraid.
What can mere mortals do to me?

5 All day long they twist my words;
all their schemes are for my ruin.
6 They conspire, they lurk,
they watch my steps,
hoping to take my life.
7 Because of their wickedness do not let them
escape;
in your anger, God, bring the nations down.

8 Record my misery;
list my tears on your scroll —
are they not in your record?
9 Then my enemies will turn back
when I call for help.
By this I will know that God is for me.

10 In God, whose word I praise,
    in the LORD, whose word I praise —
11 in God I trust and am not afraid.
    What can man do to me?

12 I am under vows to you, my God;
    I will present my thank offerings to you.
13 For you have delivered me from death
    and my feet from stumbling,
that I may walk before God
    in the light of life.

PSALM 57

*For the director of music. To the tune
of "Do Not Destroy." Of David. A miktam. When
he had fled from Saul into the cave.*

1   Have mercy on me, my God, have mercy
        on me,
     for in you I take refuge.
   I will take refuge in the shadow of your wings
     until the disaster has passed.

2   I cry out to God Most High,
     to God, who vindicates me.
3   He sends from heaven and saves me,
     rebuking those who hotly pursue me —
   God sends forth his love and his
     faithfulness.

4   I am in the midst of lions;
     I am forced to dwell among ravenous
       beasts —
   men whose teeth are spears and arrows,
     whose tongues are sharp swords.

5   Be exalted, O God, above the heavens;
     let your glory be over all the earth.

6   They spread a net for my feet —
     I was bowed down in distress.
   They dug a pit in my path —
     but they have fallen into it themselves.

7　My heart, O God, is steadfast,
　　　　my heart is steadfast;
　　　　I will sing and make music.

8　Awake, my soul!
　　　　Awake, harp and lyre!
　　　　I will awaken the dawn.

9　I will praise you, Lord, among the nations;
　　　　I will sing of you among the peoples.

10　For great is your love, reaching to the heavens;
　　　　your faithfulness reaches to the skies.

11　Be exalted, O God, above the heavens;
　　　　let your glory be over all the earth.

PSALM 58

For the director of music. To the tune of "Do Not Destroy." Of David. A miktam.

1   Do you rulers indeed speak justly?
     Do you judge people with equity?
2   No, in your heart you devise injustice,
     and your hands mete out violence on the
       earth.

3   Even from birth the wicked go astray;
     from the womb they are wayward, spreading
       lies.
4   Their venom is like the venom of a snake,
     like that of a cobra that has stopped its ears,
5   that will not heed the tune of the charmer,
     however skillful the enchanter may be.

6   Break the teeth in their mouths, O God;
     LORD, tear out the fangs of those lions!
7   Let them vanish like water that flows away;
     when they draw the bow, let their arrows fall
       short.
8   May they be like a slug that melts away as it
       moves along,
     like a stillborn child that never sees the sun.

9   Before your pots can feel the heat of the
       thorns—
     whether they be green or dry—the wicked
       will be swept away.

10   The righteous will be glad when they are
              avenged,
          when they dip their feet in the blood
              of the wicked.
11   Then people will say,
          "Surely the righteous still are rewarded;
          surely there is a God who judges the
              earth."

PSALM 59

For the director of music. To the tune of "Do Not Destroy." Of David. A miktam. When Saul had sent men to watch David's house in order to kill him.

1 Deliver me from my enemies, O God;
    be my fortress against those who are
        attacking me.
2 Deliver me from evildoers
    and save me from those who are after my
        blood.

3 See how they lie in wait for me!
    Fierce men conspire against me
    for no offense or sin of mine, Lord.
4 I have done no wrong, yet they are ready to
        attack me.
    Arise to help me; look on my plight!
5 You, Lord God Almighty,
    you who are the God of Israel,
  rouse yourself to punish all the nations;
    show no mercy to wicked traitors.

6 They return at evening,
    snarling like dogs,
    and prowl about the city.
7 See what they spew from their mouths —
    the words from their lips are sharp as
        swords,
    and they think, "Who can hear us?"

8   But you laugh at them, LORD;
       you scoff at all those nations.

9   You are my strength, I watch for you;
       you, God, are my fortress,
10   my God on whom I can rely.

     God will go before me
       and will let me gloat over those who slander
         me.
11   But do not kill them, Lord our shield,
       or my people will forget.
     In your might uproot them
       and bring them down.
12   For the sins of their mouths,
       for the words of their lips,
         let them be caught in their pride.
     For the curses and lies they utter,
13   consume them in your wrath,
         consume them till they are no more.
     Then it will be known to the ends of the earth
       that God rules over Jacob.

14   They return at evening,
       snarling like dogs,
         and prowl about the city.
15   They wander about for food
       and howl if not satisfied.
16   But I will sing of your strength,
       in the morning I will sing of your love;
     for you are my fortress,
       my refuge in times of trouble.

17   You are my strength, I sing praise to you;
        you, God, are my fortress,
        my God on whom I can rely.

PSALM 60

For the director of music. To the tune of "The Lily of the Covenant." A miktam of David. For teaching. When he fought Aram Naharaim and Aram Zobah, and when Joab returned and struck down twelve thousand Edomites in the Valley of Salt.

1   You have rejected us, God, and burst
        upon us;
            you have been angry — now restore us!
2   You have shaken the land and torn it open;
        mend its fractures, for it is quaking.
3   You have shown your people desperate times;
        you have given us wine that makes us
            stagger.
4   But for those who fear you, you have raised a
        banner
            to be unfurled against the bow.

5   Save us and help us with your right hand,
        that those you love may be delivered.
6   God has spoken from his sanctuary:
        "In triumph I will parcel out Shechem
        and measure off the Valley of Sukkoth.
7   Gilead is mine, and Manasseh is mine;
        Ephraim is my helmet,
        Judah is my scepter.
8   Moab is my washbasin,
        on Edom I toss my sandal;
        over Philistia I shout in triumph."

9 Who will bring me to the fortified city?
     Who will lead me to Edom?
10 Is it not you, God, you who have now
          rejected us
     and no longer go out with our armies?
11 Give us aid against the enemy,
     for human help is worthless.
12 With God we will gain the victory,
     and he will trample down our enemies.

PSALM 61

*For the director of music. With stringed
instruments. Of David.*

1 Hear my cry, O God;
  listen to my prayer.

2 From the ends of the earth I call to you,
  I call as my heart grows faint;
  lead me to the rock that is higher than I.

3 For you have been my refuge,
  a strong tower against the foe.

4 I long to dwell in your tent forever
  and take refuge in the shelter of your wings.

5 For you, God, have heard my vows;
  you have given me the heritage of those who
    fear your name.

6 Increase the days of the king's life,
  his years for many generations.

7 May he be enthroned in God's presence forever;
  appoint your love and faithfulness to protect
    him.

8 Then I will ever sing in praise of your name
  and fulfill my vows day after day.

PSALM 62

For the director of music. For Jeduthun.
A psalm of David.

1   Truly my soul finds rest in God;
  my salvation comes from him.
2   Truly he is my rock and my salvation;
  he is my fortress, I will never be
   shaken.

3   How long will you assault me?
  Would all of you throw me down —
  this leaning wall, this tottering
   fence?
4   Surely they intend to topple me
  from my lofty place;
  they take delight in lies.
 With their mouths they bless,
  but in their hearts they curse.

5   Yes, my soul, find rest in God;
  my hope comes from him.
6   Truly he is my rock and my salvation;
  he is my fortress, I will not be shaken.
7   My salvation and my honor depend on
   God;
  he is my mighty rock, my refuge.
8   Trust in him at all times, you people;
  pour out your hearts to him,
  for God is our refuge.

9   Surely the lowborn are but a breath,
      the highborn are but a lie.
    If weighed on a balance, they are nothing;
      together they are only a breath.

10   Do not trust in extortion
      or put vain hope in stolen goods;
    though your riches increase,
      do not set your heart on them.

11   One thing God has spoken,
      two things I have heard:
    "Power belongs to you, God,
12   and with you, Lord, is unfailing love";
    and, "You reward everyone
      according to what they have done."

PSALM 63

A psalm of David. When he was in the Desert of Judah.

1   You, God, are my God,
        earnestly I seek you;
    I thirst for you,
        my whole being longs for you,
    in a dry and parched land
        where there is no water.

2   I have seen you in the sanctuary
        and beheld your power and your glory.
3   Because your love is better than life,
        my lips will glorify you.
4   I will praise you as long as I live,
        and in your name I will lift up my hands.
5   I will be fully satisfied as with the richest of
                foods;
        with singing lips my mouth will praise you.

6   On my bed I remember you;
        I think of you through the watches of the
                night.
7   Because you are my help,
        I sing in the shadow of your wings.
8   I cling to you;
        your right hand upholds me.

9   Those who want to kill me will be destroyed;
        they will go down to the depths of the earth.

10   They will be given over to the sword
       and become food for jackals.

11   But the king will rejoice in God;
       all who swear by God will glory in him,
       while the mouths of liars will be silenced.

PSALM 64

For the director of music. A psalm of David.

1   Hear me, my God, as I voice my complaint;
        protect my life from the threat of the enemy.

2   Hide me from the conspiracy of the wicked,
        from the plots of evildoers.
3   They sharpen their tongues like swords
        and aim cruel words like deadly arrows.
4   They shoot from ambush at the innocent;
        they shoot suddenly, without fear.

5   They encourage each other in evil plans,
        they talk about hiding their snares;
        they say, "Who will see it?"
6   They plot injustice and say,
        "We have devised a perfect plan!"
        Surely the human mind and heart are
            cunning.

7   But God will shoot them with his arrows;
        they will suddenly be struck down.
8   He will turn their own tongues against them
        and bring them to ruin;
        all who see them will shake their heads in
            scorn.
9   All people will fear;
        they will proclaim the works of God
        and ponder what he has done.

10   The righteous will rejoice in the LORD
        and take refuge in him;
        all the upright in heart will glory in him!

PSALM 65

For the director of music. A psalm of David. A song.

1 Praise awaits you, our God, in Zion;
  to you our vows will be fulfilled.
2 You who answer prayer,
  to you all people will come.
3 When we were overwhelmed by sins,
  you forgave our transgressions.
4 Blessed are those you choose
  and bring near to live in your courts!
  We are filled with the good things of your
      house,
  of your holy temple.

5 You answer us with awesome and righteous
      deeds,
  God our Savior,
  the hope of all the ends of the earth
  and of the farthest seas,
6 who formed the mountains by your power,
  having armed yourself with strength,
7 who stilled the roaring of the seas,
  the roaring of their waves,
  and the turmoil of the nations.
8 The whole earth is filled with awe at your
      wonders;
  where morning dawns, where evening fades,
  you call forth songs of joy.

9   You care for the land and water it;
         you enrich it abundantly.
      The streams of God are filled with water
         to provide the people with grain,
         for so you have ordained it.
10   You drench its furrows and level its ridges;
         you soften it with showers and bless its
            crops.
11   You crown the year with your bounty,
         and your carts overflow with abundance.
12   The grasslands of the wilderness overflow;
         the hills are clothed with gladness.
13   The meadows are covered with flocks
         and the valleys are mantled with grain;
         they shout for joy and sing.

PSALM 66

For the director of music. A song. A psalm.

1 Shout for joy to God, all the earth!
2   Sing the glory of his name;
   make his praise glorious.
3 Say to God, "How awesome are your deeds!
   So great is your power
   that your enemies cringe before you.
4 All the earth bows down to you;
   they sing praise to you,
   they sing the praises of your name."

5 Come and see what God has done,
   his awesome deeds for mankind!
6 He turned the sea into dry land,
   they passed through the waters on foot —
   come, let us rejoice in him.
7 He rules forever by his power,
   his eyes watch the nations —
   let not the rebellious rise up against him.

8 Praise our God, all peoples,
   let the sound of his praise be heard;
9 he has preserved our lives
   and kept our feet from slipping.
10 For you, God, tested us;
   you refined us like silver.
11 You brought us into prison
   and laid burdens on our backs.

12   You let people ride over our heads;
            we went through fire and water,
            but you brought us to a place of abundance.

13   I will come to your temple with burnt offerings
            and fulfill my vows to you —
14   vows my lips promised and my mouth spoke
            when I was in trouble.
15   I will sacrifice fat animals to you
            and an offering of rams;
            I will offer bulls and goats.

16   Come and hear, all you who fear God;
            let me tell you what he has done for me.
17   I cried out to him with my mouth;
            his praise was on my tongue.
18   If I had cherished sin in my heart,
            the Lord would not have listened;
19   but God has surely listened
            and has heard my prayer.
20   Praise be to God,
            who has not rejected my prayer
            or withheld his love from me!

PSALM 67

For the director of music. With stringed instruments. A psalm. A song.

1   May God be gracious to us and bless us
    and make his face shine on us —
2   so that your ways may be known on earth,
    your salvation among all nations.

3   May the peoples praise you, God;
    may all the peoples praise you.
4   May the nations be glad and sing for joy,
    for you rule the peoples with equity
    and guide the nations of the earth.
5   May the peoples praise you, God;
    may all the peoples praise you.

6   The land yields its harvest;
    God, our God, blesses us.
7   May God bless us still,
    so that all the ends of the earth will fear
    him.

PSALM 68

For the director of music. Of David.
A psalm. A song.

1   May God arise, may his enemies be scattered;
    may his foes flee before him.
2   May you blow them away like smoke —
    as wax melts before the fire,
    may the wicked perish before God.
3   But may the righteous be glad
    and rejoice before God;
    may they be happy and joyful.

4   Sing to God, sing in praise of his name,
    extol him who rides on the clouds;
    rejoice before him — his name is the Lord.
5   A father to the fatherless, a defender of
    widows,
    is God in his holy dwelling.
6   God sets the lonely in families,
    he leads out the prisoners with singing;
    but the rebellious live in a sun-scorched
    land.

7   When you, God, went out before your people,
    when you marched through the wilderness,
8   the earth shook, the heavens poured down
    rain,
    before God, the One of Sinai,
    before God, the God of Israel.

9   You gave abundant showers, O God;
       you refreshed your weary inheritance.
10   Your people settled in it,
       and from your bounty, God, you provided for
          the poor.

11   The Lord announces the word,
       and the women who proclaim it are a
          mighty throng:
12   "Kings and armies flee in haste;
       the women at home divide the plunder.
13   Even while you sleep among the sheep pens,
       the wings of my dove are sheathed with
          silver,
       its feathers with shining gold."
14   When the Almighty scattered the kings in the
          land,
       it was like snow fallen on Mount Zalmon.

15   Mount Bashan, majestic mountain,
       Mount Bashan, rugged mountain,
16   why gaze in envy, you rugged mountain,
       at the mountain where God chooses to
          reign,
       where the LORD himself will dwell forever?
17   The chariots of God are tens of thousands
       and thousands of thousands;
       the Lord has come from Sinai into his
          sanctuary.
18   When you ascended on high,
       you took many captives;
       you received gifts from people,

even from the rebellious —
>> that you, LORD God, might dwell there.

19 Praise be to the Lord, to God our Savior,
>> who daily bears our burdens.
20 Our God is a God who saves;
>> from the Sovereign LORD comes escape from death.
21 Surely God will crush the heads of his enemies,
>> the hairy crowns of those who go on in their sins.
22 The Lord says, "I will bring them from Bashan;
>> I will bring them from the depths of the sea,
23 that your feet may wade in the blood of your foes,
>> while the tongues of your dogs have their share."

24 Your procession, God, has come into view,
>> the procession of my God and King into the sanctuary.
25 In front are the singers, after them the musicians;
>> with them are the young women playing the timbrels.
26 Praise God in the great congregation;
>> praise the LORD in the assembly of Israel.
27 There is the little tribe of Benjamin, leading them,
>> there the great throng of Judah's princes,
>> and there the princes of Zebulun and of Naphtali.

28 Summon your power, God;
   show us your strength, our God, as you have
   done before.
29 Because of your temple at Jerusalem
   kings will bring you gifts.
30 Rebuke the beast among the reeds,
   the herd of bulls among the calves of the
   nations.
   Humbled, may the beast bring bars of silver.
   Scatter the nations who delight in war.
31 Envoys will come from Egypt;
   Cush will submit herself to God.

32 Sing to God, you kingdoms of the earth,
   sing praise to the Lord,
33 to him who rides across the highest heavens,
   the ancient heavens,
   who thunders with mighty voice.
34 Proclaim the power of God,
   whose majesty is over Israel,
   whose power is in the heavens.
35 You, God, are awesome in your sanctuary;
   the God of Israel gives power and strength to
   his people.

Praise be to God!

PSALM 69

For the director of music. To the tune
of "Lilies." Of David.

1 Save me, O God,
      for the waters have come up to my neck.
2 I sink in the miry depths,
      where there is no foothold.
   I have come into the deep waters;
      the floods engulf me.
3 I am worn out calling for help;
      my throat is parched.
   My eyes fail,
      looking for my God.
4 Those who hate me without reason
      outnumber the hairs of my head;
   many are my enemies without cause,
      those who seek to destroy me.
   I am forced to restore
      what I did not steal.

5 You, God, know my folly;
      my guilt is not hidden from you.

6 Lord, the Lord Almighty,
      may those who hope in you
      not be disgraced because of me;
   God of Israel,
      may those who seek you
      not be put to shame because of me.

7 For I endure scorn for your sake,
       and shame covers my face.
8 I am a foreigner to my own family,
       a stranger to my own mother's
           children;
9 for zeal for your house consumes me,
       and the insults of those who insult you
           fall on me.
10 When I weep and fast,
       I must endure scorn;
11 when I put on sackcloth,
       people make sport of me.
12 Those who sit at the gate mock me,
       and I am the song of the drunkards.

13 But I pray to you, LORD,
       in the time of your favor;
   in your great love, O God,
       answer me with your sure salvation.
14 Rescue me from the mire,
       do not let me sink;
   deliver me from those who hate me,
       from the deep waters.
15 Do not let the floodwaters engulf me
       or the depths swallow me up
       or the pit close its mouth over me.

16 Answer me, LORD, out of the goodness
           of your love;
       in your great mercy turn to me.
17 Do not hide your face from your servant;
       answer me quickly, for I am in trouble.

18 Come near and rescue me;
      deliver me because of my foes.

19 You know how I am scorned, disgraced and
            shamed;
      all my enemies are before you.

20 Scorn has broken my heart
      and has left me helpless;
   I looked for sympathy, but there was none,
      for comforters, but I found none.

21 They put gall in my food
      and gave me vinegar for my thirst.

22 May the table set before them become a snare;
      may it become retribution and a trap.

23 May their eyes be darkened so they cannot see,
      and their backs be bent forever.

24 Pour out your wrath on them;
      let your fierce anger overtake them.

25 May their place be deserted;
      let there be no one to dwell in their tents.

26 For they persecute those you wound
      and talk about the pain of those you hurt.

27 Charge them with crime upon crime;
      do not let them share in your salvation.

28 May they be blotted out of the book of life
      and not be listed with the righteous.

29 But as for me, afflicted and in pain —
      may your salvation, God, protect me.

30 I will praise God's name in song
      and glorify him with thanksgiving.

31 This will please the LORD more than an ox,
   more than a bull with its horns and hooves.
32 The poor will see and be glad —
   you who seek God, may your hearts live!
33 The LORD hears the needy
   and does not despise his captive people.

34 Let heaven and earth praise him,
   the seas and all that move in them,
35 for God will save Zion
   and rebuild the cities of Judah.
  Then people will settle there and possess it;
36 the children of his servants will inherit it,
   and those who love his name will dwell there.

PSALM 70

For the director of music. Of David. A petition.

1 Hasten, O God, to save me;
    come quickly, LORD, to help me.

2 May those who want to take my life
    be put to shame and confusion;
  may all who desire my ruin
    be turned back in disgrace.

3 May those who say to me, "Aha! Aha!"
    turn back because of their shame.

4 But may all who seek you
    rejoice and be glad in you;
  may those who long for your saving help
      always say,
    "The LORD is great!"

5 But as for me, I am poor and needy;
    come quickly to me, O God.
  You are my help and my deliverer;
    LORD, do not delay.

PSALM 71

1   In you, Lord, I have taken refuge;
   let me never be put to shame.
2   In your righteousness, rescue me and
      deliver me;
   turn your ear to me and save me.
3   Be my rock of refuge,
   to which I can always go;
 give the command to save me,
   for you are my rock and my fortress.
4   Deliver me, my God, from the hand of the
      wicked,
   from the grasp of those who are evil and
      cruel.

5   For you have been my hope, Sovereign Lord,
   my confidence since my youth.
6   From birth I have relied on you;
   you brought me forth from my mother's
      womb.
   I will ever praise you.
7   I have become a sign to many;
   you are my strong refuge.
8   My mouth is filled with your praise,
   declaring your splendor all day long.

9   Do not cast me away when I am old;
   do not forsake me when my strength is
      gone.

10 For my enemies speak against me;
        those who wait to kill me conspire together.
11 They say, "God has forsaken him;
        pursue him and seize him,
        for no one will rescue him."
12 Do not be far from me, my God;
        come quickly, God, to help me.
13 May my accusers perish in shame;
        may those who want to harm me
        be covered with scorn and disgrace.

14 As for me, I will always have hope;
        I will praise you more and more.

15 My mouth will tell of your righteous deeds,
        of your saving acts all day long —
        though I know not how to relate them all.
16 I will come and proclaim your mighty acts,
        Sovereign LORD;
        I will proclaim your righteous deeds, yours
        alone.
17 Since my youth, God, you have taught me,
        and to this day I declare your marvelous
        deeds.
18 Even when I am old and gray,
        do not forsake me, my God,
    till I declare your power to the next generation,
        your mighty acts to all who are to come.

19 Your righteousness, God, reaches to the
        heavens,
        you who have done great things.
        Who is like you, God?

20   Though you have made me see troubles,
       many and bitter,
       you will restore my life again;
    from the depths of the earth
       you will again bring me up.
21   You will increase my honor
       and comfort me once more.

22   I will praise you with the harp
       for your faithfulness, my God;
    I will sing praise to you with the lyre,
       Holy One of Israel.
23   My lips will shout for joy
       when I sing praise to you —
       I whom you have delivered.
24   My tongue will tell of your righteous acts
       all day long,
    for those who wanted to harm me
       have been put to shame and confusion.

PSALM 72

Of Solomon.

1   Endow the king with your justice, O God,
        the royal son with your righteousness.
2   May he judge your people in righteousness,
        your afflicted ones with justice.

3   May the mountains bring prosperity to the
           people,
        the hills the fruit of righteousness.
4   May he defend the afflicted among the people
        and save the children of the needy;
        may he crush the oppressor.
5   May he endure as long as the sun,
        as long as the moon, through all generations.
6   May he be like rain falling on a mown field,
        like showers watering the earth.
7   In his days may the righteous flourish
        and prosperity abound till the moon is no
           more.

8   May he rule from sea to sea
        and from the River to the ends of the earth.
9   May the desert tribes bow before him
        and his enemies lick the dust.
10   May the kings of Tarshish and of distant shores
        bring tribute to him.
      May the kings of Sheba and Seba
        present him gifts.

11   May all kings bow down to him
         and all nations serve him.

12   For he will deliver the needy who cry out,
         the afflicted who have no one to help.
13   He will take pity on the weak and the needy
         and save the needy from death.
14   He will rescue them from oppression and
              violence,
         for precious is their blood in his sight.

15   Long may he live!
         May gold from Sheba be given him.
     May people ever pray for him
         and bless him all day long.
16   May grain abound throughout the land;
         on the tops of the hills may it sway.
     May the crops flourish like Lebanon
         and thrive like the grass of the field.
17   May his name endure forever;
         may it continue as long as the sun.

     Then all nations will be blessed through him,
         and they will call him blessed.

18   Praise be to the Lord God, the God of Israel,
         who alone does marvelous deeds.
19   Praise be to his glorious name forever;
         may the whole earth be filled with his glory.
              Amen and Amen.

20   This concludes the prayers of David son
         of Jesse.

BOOK III

Psalms 73–89

PSALM 73

A psalm of Asaph.

1   Surely God is good to Israel,
        to those who are pure in heart.

2   But as for me, my feet had almost slipped;
        I had nearly lost my foothold.

3   For I envied the arrogant
        when I saw the prosperity of the
            wicked.

4   They have no struggles;
        their bodies are healthy and strong.

5   They are free from common human
            burdens;
        they are not plagued by human ills.

6   Therefore pride is their necklace;
        they clothe themselves with violence.

7   From their callous hearts comes iniquity;
        their evil imaginations have no limits.

8   They scoff, and speak with malice;
        with arrogance they threaten oppression.

9   Their mouths lay claim to heaven,
        and their tongues take possession of
            the earth.

10 Therefore their people turn to them
        and drink up waters in abundance.

11 They say, "How would God know?
        Does the Most High know anything?"

12 This is what the wicked are like —
        always free of care, they go on amassing
            wealth.

13 Surely in vain I have kept my heart pure
        and have washed my hands in innocence.

14 All day long I have been afflicted,
        and every morning brings new
            punishments.

15 If I had spoken out like that,
        I would have betrayed your children.

16 When I tried to understand all this,
        it troubled me deeply

17 till I entered the sanctuary of God;
        then I understood their final destiny.

18 Surely you place them on slippery ground;
        you cast them down to ruin.

19 How suddenly are they destroyed,
        completely swept away by terrors!

20 They are like a dream when one awakes;
        when you arise, Lord,
            you will despise them as fantasies.

21 When my heart was grieved
        and my spirit embittered,

22 I was senseless and ignorant;
        I was a brute beast before you.

23 Yet I am always with you;
        you hold me by my right hand.

24 You guide me with your counsel,
        and afterward you will take me into glory.

25 Whom have I in heaven but you?
   And earth has nothing I desire besides you.
26 My flesh and my heart may fail,
   but God is the strength of my heart
   and my portion forever.

27 Those who are far from you will perish;
   you destroy all who are unfaithful to you.
28 But as for me, it is good to be near God.
   I have made the Sovereign LORD my refuge;
   I will tell of all your deeds.

PSALM 74

1 O God, why have you rejected us forever?
Why does your anger smolder against the
sheep of your pasture?
2 Remember the nation you purchased long ago,
the people of your inheritance, whom you
redeemed —
Mount Zion, where you dwelt.
3 Turn your steps toward these everlasting
ruins,
all this destruction the enemy has brought
on the sanctuary.

4 Your foes roared in the place where you met
with us;
they set up their standards as signs.
5 They behaved like men wielding axes
to cut through a thicket of trees.
6 They smashed all the carved paneling
with their axes and hatchets.
7 They burned your sanctuary to the ground;
they defiled the dwelling place of your
Name.
8 They said in their hearts, "We will crush them
completely!"
They burned every place where God was
worshiped in the land.

9   We are given no signs from God;
        no prophets are left,
        and none of us knows how long this will be.

10   How long will the enemy mock you, God?
        Will the foe revile your name forever?

11   Why do you hold back your hand, your right
        hand?
        Take it from the folds of your garment and
        destroy them!

12   But God is my King from long ago;
        he brings salvation on the earth.

13   It was you who split open the sea by your
        power;
        you broke the heads of the monster in the
        waters.

14   It was you who crushed the heads of
        Leviathan
        and gave it as food to the creatures of the
        desert.

15   It was you who opened up springs and
        streams;
        you dried up the ever-flowing rivers.

16   The day is yours, and yours also the night;
        you established the sun and moon.

17   It was you who set all the boundaries of the
        earth;
        you made both summer and winter.

18   Remember how the enemy has mocked you,
        LORD,
        how foolish people have reviled your name.

19   Do not hand over the life of your dove to wild
         beasts;
       do not forget the lives of your afflicted
         people forever.

20   Have regard for your covenant,
       because haunts of violence fill the dark
         places of the land.

21   Do not let the oppressed retreat in disgrace;
       may the poor and needy praise your name.

22   Rise up, O God, and defend your cause;
       remember how fools mock you all day long.

23   Do not ignore the clamor of your adversaries,
       the uproar of your enemies, which rises
         continually.

PSALM 75

*For the director of music. To the tune
of "Do Not Destroy." A psalm of Asaph.
A song.*

1 We praise you, God,
  we praise you, for your Name is near;
  people tell of your wonderful deeds.

2 You say, "I choose the appointed time;
  it is I who judge with equity.

3 When the earth and all its people quake,
  it is I who hold its pillars firm.

4 To the arrogant I say, 'Boast no more,'
  and to the wicked, 'Do not lift up your
      horns.

5 Do not lift your horns against heaven;
  do not speak so defiantly.'"

6 No one from the east or the west
  or from the desert can exalt themselves.

7 It is God who judges:
  He brings one down, he exalts another.

8 In the hand of the LORD is a cup
  full of foaming wine mixed with spices;
  he pours it out, and all the wicked of the
      earth
  drink it down to its very dregs.

9 As for me, I will declare this forever;
  I will sing praise to the God of Jacob,

10   who says, "I will cut off the horns of all the
               wicked,
        but the horns of the righteous will be
             lifted up."

PSALM 76

*For the director of music. With stringed
instruments. A psalm of Asaph. A song.*

1 God is renowned in Judah;
    in Israel his name is great.
2 His tent is in Salem,
    his dwelling place in Zion.
3 There he broke the flashing arrows,
    the shields and the swords, the weapons
        of war.

4 You are radiant with light,
    more majestic than mountains rich
        with game.
5 The valiant lie plundered,
    they sleep their last sleep;
not one of the warriors
    can lift his hands.
6 At your rebuke, God of Jacob,
    both horse and chariot lie still.

7 It is you alone who are to be feared.
    Who can stand before you when you
        are angry?
8 From heaven you pronounced judgment,
    and the land feared and was
        quiet —
9 when you, God, rose up to judge,
    to save all the afflicted of the land.

10   Surely your wrath against mankind brings you
              praise,
          and the survivors of your wrath are
              restrained.

11   Make vows to the LORD your God and fulfill
              them;
          let all the neighboring lands
          bring gifts to the One to be feared.
12   He breaks the spirit of rulers;
          he is feared by the kings of the earth.

PSALM 77

For the director of music. For Jeduthun.
Of Asaph. A psalm.

1 I cried out to God for help;
   I cried out to God to hear me.
2 When I was in distress, I sought the Lord;
   at night I stretched out untiring hands,
   and I would not be comforted.

3 I remembered you, God, and I groaned;
   I meditated, and my spirit grew faint.
4 You kept my eyes from closing;
   I was too troubled to speak.
5 I thought about the former days,
   the years of long ago;
6 I remembered my songs in the night.
   My heart meditated and my spirit
      asked:

7 "Will the Lord reject forever?
   Will he never show his favor again?
8 Has his unfailing love vanished forever?
   Has his promise failed for all time?
9 Has God forgotten to be merciful?
   Has he in anger withheld his compassion?"

10 Then I thought, "To this I will appeal:
    the years when the Most High stretched
       out his right hand.

11 I will remember the deeds of the LORD;
   yes, I will remember your miracles of long
      ago.
12 I will consider all your works
   and meditate on all your mighty deeds."

13 Your ways, God, are holy.
   What god is as great as our God?
14 You are the God who performs miracles;
   you display your power among the peoples.
15 With your mighty arm you redeemed your
      people,
   the descendants of Jacob and Joseph.

16 The waters saw you, God,
   the waters saw you and writhed;
   the very depths were convulsed.
17 The clouds poured down water,
   the heavens resounded with thunder;
   your arrows flashed back and forth.
18 Your thunder was heard in the whirlwind,
   your lightning lit up the world;
   the earth trembled and quaked.
19 Your path led through the sea,
   your way through the mighty waters,
   though your footprints were not seen.

20 You led your people like a flock
   by the hand of Moses and Aaron.

PSALM 78

A maskil of Asaph.

1 My people, hear my teaching;
   listen to the words of my mouth.
2 I will open my mouth with a parable;
   I will utter hidden things, things from
      of old —
3 things we have heard and known,
   things our ancestors have told us.
4 We will not hide them from their
      descendants;
   we will tell the next generation
the praiseworthy deeds of the Lord,
   his power, and the wonders he has done.
5 He decreed statutes for Jacob
   and established the law in Israel,
which he commanded our ancestors
   to teach their children,
6 so the next generation would know them,
   even the children yet to be born,
   and they in turn would tell their children.
7 Then they would put their trust in God
   and would not forget his deeds
   but would keep his commands.
8 They would not be like their ancestors —
   a stubborn and rebellious generation,
whose hearts were not loyal to God,
   whose spirits were not faithful to him.

9   The men of Ephraim, though armed with
         bows,
        turned back on the day of battle;
10   they did not keep God's covenant
        and refused to live by his law.
11   They forgot what he had done,
        the wonders he had shown them.
12   He did miracles in the sight of their ancestors
        in the land of Egypt, in the region of Zoan.
13   He divided the sea and led them through;
        he made the water stand up like a wall.
14   He guided them with the cloud by day
        and with light from the fire all night.
15   He split the rocks in the wilderness
        and gave them water as abundant as the
         seas;
16   he brought streams out of a rocky crag
        and made water flow down like rivers.

17   But they continued to sin against him,
        rebelling in the wilderness against the
         Most High.
18   They willfully put God to the test
        by demanding the food they craved.
19   They spoke against God;
        they said, "Can God really
        spread a table in the wilderness?
20   True, he struck the rock,
        and water gushed out,
        streams flowed abundantly,
     but can he also give us bread?
        Can he supply meat for his people?"

21 When the L ORD heard them, he was furious;
     his fire broke out against Jacob,
     and his wrath rose against Israel,
22 for they did not believe in God
     or trust in his deliverance.
23 Yet he gave a command to the skies above
     and opened the doors of the heavens;
24 he rained down manna for the people to eat,
     he gave them the grain of heaven.
25 Human beings ate the bread of angels;
     he sent them all the food they could eat.
26 He let loose the east wind from the heavens
     and by his power made the south wind
          blow.
27 He rained meat down on them like dust,
     birds like sand on the seashore.
28 He made them come down inside their camp,
     all around their tents.
29 They ate till they were gorged —
     he had given them what they craved.
30 But before they turned from what they
          craved,
     even while the food was still in their
          mouths,
31 God's anger rose against them;
     he put to death the sturdiest among them,
     cutting down the young men of Israel.

32 In spite of all this, they kept on sinning;
     in spite of his wonders, they did not believe.
33 So he ended their days in futility
     and their years in terror.

34 Whenever God slew them, they would seek
     him;
    they eagerly turned to him again.
35 They remembered that God was their Rock,
    that God Most High was their Redeemer.
36 But then they would flatter him with their
     mouths,
    lying to him with their tongues;
37 their hearts were not loyal to him,
    they were not faithful to his covenant.
38 Yet he was merciful;
    he forgave their iniquities
    and did not destroy them.
Time after time he restrained his anger
    and did not stir up his full wrath.
39 He remembered that they were but flesh,
    a passing breeze that does not return.

40 How often they rebelled against him in the
     wilderness
    and grieved him in the wasteland!
41 Again and again they put God to the test;
    they vexed the Holy One of Israel.
42 They did not remember his power—
    the day he redeemed them from the
     oppressor,
43 the day he displayed his signs in Egypt,
    his wonders in the region of Zoan.
44 He turned their river into blood;
    they could not drink from their streams.
45 He sent swarms of flies that devoured them,
    and frogs that devastated them.

46 He gave their crops to the grasshopper,
      their produce to the locust.
47 He destroyed their vines with hail
      and their sycamore-figs with sleet.
48 He gave over their cattle to the hail,
      their livestock to bolts of lightning.
49 He unleashed against them his hot anger,
      his wrath, indignation and hostility —
      a band of destroying angels.
50 He prepared a path for his anger;
      he did not spare them from death
      but gave them over to the plague.
51 He struck down all the firstborn of Egypt,
      the firstfruits of manhood in the tents of
         Ham.
52 But he brought his people out like a flock;
      he led them like sheep through the
         wilderness.
53 He guided them safely, so they were unafraid;
      but the sea engulfed their enemies.
54 And so he brought them to the border of his
         holy land,
      to the hill country his right hand had taken.
55 He drove out nations before them
      and allotted their lands to them as an
         inheritance;
      he settled the tribes of Israel in their
         homes.

56 But they put God to the test
      and rebelled against the Most High;
      they did not keep his statutes.

57 Like their ancestors they were disloyal and
    faithless,
    as unreliable as a faulty bow.
58 They angered him with their high places;
    they aroused his jealousy with their idols.
59 When God heard them, he was furious;
    he rejected Israel completely.
60 He abandoned the tabernacle of Shiloh,
    the tent he had set up among humans.
61 He sent the ark of his might into captivity,
    his splendor into the hands of the enemy.
62 He gave his people over to the sword;
    he was furious with his inheritance.
63 Fire consumed their young men,
    and their young women had no wedding
    songs;
64 their priests were put to the sword,
    and their widows could not weep.

65 Then the Lord awoke as from sleep,
    as a warrior wakes from the stupor of
    wine.
66 He beat back his enemies;
    he put them to everlasting shame.
67 Then he rejected the tents of Joseph,
    he did not choose the tribe of Ephraim;
68 but he chose the tribe of Judah,
    Mount Zion, which he loved.
69 He built his sanctuary like the heights,
    like the earth that he established forever.
70 He chose David his servant
    and took him from the sheep pens;

71   from tending the sheep he brought him
         to be the shepherd of his people Jacob,
         of Israel his inheritance.
72   And David shepherded them with integrity of
              heart;
         with skillful hands he led them.

PSALM 79

A psalm of Asaph.

1   O God, the nations have invaded your
        inheritance;
        they have defiled your holy temple,
        they have reduced Jerusalem to rubble.
2   They have left the dead bodies of your servants
        as food for the birds of the sky,
        the flesh of your own people for the animals
            of the wild.
3   They have poured out blood like water
        all around Jerusalem,
        and there is no one to bury the dead.
4   We are objects of contempt to our neighbors,
        of scorn and derision to those around us.

5   How long, LORD? Will you be angry forever?
        How long will your jealousy burn like fire?
6   Pour out your wrath on the nations
        that do not acknowledge you,
    on the kingdoms
        that do not call on your name;
7   for they have devoured Jacob
        and devastated his homeland.

8   Do not hold against us the sins of past
        generations;
        may your mercy come quickly to meet us,
        for we are in desperate need.

9   Help us, God our Savior,
         for the glory of your name;
     deliver us and forgive our sins
         for your name's sake.

10   Why should the nations say,
         "Where is their God?"

     Before our eyes, make known among the
             nations
         that you avenge the outpoured blood of
             your servants.

11   May the groans of the prisoners come before
             you;
         with your strong arm preserve those
             condemned to die.

12   Pay back into the laps of our neighbors seven
             times
         the contempt they have hurled at you, Lord.

13   Then we your people, the sheep of your
             pasture,
         will praise you forever;
     from generation to generation
         we will proclaim your praise.

PSALM 80

*For the director of music. To the tune
of "The Lilies of the Covenant." Of Asaph.
A psalm.*

1   Hear us, Shepherd of Israel,
        you who lead Joseph like a flock.
    You who sit enthroned between the
            cherubim,
        shine forth
2   before Ephraim, Benjamin and Manasseh.
    Awaken your might;
        come and save us.

3   Restore us, O God;
        make your face shine on us,
        that we may be saved.

4   How long, Lord God Almighty,
        will your anger smolder
        against the prayers of your people?
5   You have fed them with the bread of tears;
        you have made them drink tears by the
            bowlful.
6   You have made us an object of derision to
            our neighbors,
        and our enemies mock us.

7   Restore us, God Almighty;
        make your face shine on us,
        that we may be saved.

8   You transplanted a vine from Egypt;
         you drove out the nations and planted it.
9   You cleared the ground for it,
         and it took root and filled the land.
10   The mountains were covered with its shade,
         the mighty cedars with its branches.
11   Its branches reached as far as the Sea,
         its shoots as far as the River.

12   Why have you broken down its walls
         so that all who pass by pick its grapes?
13   Boars from the forest ravage it,
         and insects from the fields feed on it.
14   Return to us, God Almighty!
         Look down from heaven and see!
     Watch over this vine,
15   the root your right hand has planted,
         the son you have raised up for yourself.

16   Your vine is cut down, it is burned with fire;
         at your rebuke your people perish.
17   Let your hand rest on the man at your right
             hand,
         the son of man you have raised up for
             yourself.
18   Then we will not turn away from you;
         revive us, and we will call on your name.

19   Restore us, LORD God Almighty;
         make your face shine on us,
         that we may be saved.

PSALM 81

For the director of music. According to gittith. *Of Asaph.*

1   Sing for joy to God our strength;
         shout aloud to the God of Jacob!
2   Begin the music, strike the timbrel,
         play the melodious harp and lyre.

3   Sound the ram's horn at the New Moon,
         and when the moon is full, on the day of our
            festival;
4   this is a decree for Israel,
         an ordinance of the God of Jacob.
5   When God went out against Egypt,
         he established it as a statute for Joseph.

    I heard an unknown voice say:

6   "I removed the burden from their shoulders;
         their hands were set free from the basket.
7   In your distress you called and I rescued you,
         I answered you out of a thundercloud;
         I tested you at the waters of Meribah.
8   Hear me, my people, and I will warn you —
         if you would only listen to me, Israel!
9   You shall have no foreign god among you;
         you shall not worship any god other than me.
10 I am the LORD your God,
         who brought you up out of Egypt.
    Open wide your mouth and I will fill it.

11   "But my people would not listen to me;
        Israel would not submit to me.
12   So I gave them over to their stubborn
                hearts
        to follow their own devices.

13   "If my people would only listen to me,
        if Israel would only follow my ways,
14   how quickly I would subdue their enemies
        and turn my hand against their foes!
15   Those who hate the LORD would cringe
                before him,
        and their punishment would last forever.
16   But you would be fed with the finest of wheat;
        with honey from the rock I would satisfy
                you."

PSALM 82

A psalm of Asaph.

1   God presides in the great assembly;
        he renders judgment among the "gods":

2   "How long will you defend the unjust
        and show partiality to the wicked?
3   Defend the weak and the fatherless;
        uphold the cause of the poor and the
           oppressed.
4   Rescue the weak and the needy;
        deliver them from the hand of the wicked.

5   "The 'gods' know nothing, they understand
           nothing.
    They walk about in darkness;
        all the foundations of the earth are
           shaken.

6   "I said, 'You are "gods";
        you are all sons of the Most High.'
7   But you will die like mere mortals;
        you will fall like every other ruler."

8   Rise up, O God, judge the earth,
        for all the nations are your inheritance.

PSALM 83

A song. A psalm of Asaph.

1   O God, do not remain silent;
    do not turn a deaf ear,
    do not stand aloof, O God.
2   See how your enemies growl,
    how your foes rear their heads.
3   With cunning they conspire against your
        people;
    they plot against those you cherish.
4   "Come," they say, "let us destroy them as a
        nation,
    so that Israel's name is remembered no
        more."

5   With one mind they plot together;
    they form an alliance against you —
6   the tents of Edom and the Ishmaelites,
    of Moab and the Hagrites,
7   Byblos, Ammon and Amalek,
    Philistia, with the people of Tyre.
8   Even Assyria has joined them
    to reinforce Lot's descendants.

9   Do to them as you did to Midian,
    as you did to Sisera and Jabin at the river
        Kishon,
10 who perished at Endor
    and became like dung on the ground.

11   Make their nobles like Oreb and Zeeb,
          all their princes like Zebah and Zalmunna,
12   who said, "Let us take possession
          of the pasturelands of God."

13   Make them like tumbleweed, my God,
          like chaff before the wind.
14   As fire consumes the forest
          or a flame sets the mountains ablaze,
15   so pursue them with your tempest
          and terrify them with your storm.
16   Cover their faces with shame, LORD,
          so that they will seek your name.

17   May they ever be ashamed and dismayed;
          may they perish in disgrace.
18   Let them know that you, whose name is the
          LORD —
          that you alone are the Most High over all the
          earth.

PSALM 84

For the director of music. According to gittith.
Of the Sons of Korah. A psalm.

1 How lovely is your dwelling place,
　　Lord Almighty!
2 My soul yearns, even faints,
　　for the courts of the Lord;
my heart and my flesh cry out
　　for the living God.
3 Even the sparrow has found a home,
　　and the swallow a nest for herself,
　　where she may have her young —
a place near your altar,
　　Lord Almighty, my King and my God.
4 Blessed are those who dwell in your house;
　　they are ever praising you.

5 Blessed are those whose strength is in you,
　　whose hearts are set on pilgrimage.
6 As they pass through the Valley of Baka,
　　they make it a place of springs;
　　the autumn rains also cover it with pools.
7 They go from strength to strength,
　　till each appears before God in Zion.

8 Hear my prayer, Lord God Almighty;
　　listen to me, God of Jacob.
9 Look on our shield, O God;
　　look with favor on your anointed one.

10   Better is one day in your courts
      than a thousand elsewhere;
   I would rather be a doorkeeper in the house of
      my God
      than dwell in the tents of the wicked.

11   For the Lord God is a sun and shield;
      the Lord bestows favor and honor;
   no good thing does he withhold
      from those whose walk is blameless.

12   Lord Almighty,
      blessed is the one who trusts in you.

PSALM 85

*For the director of music. Of the Sons
of Korah. A psalm.*

1 You, LORD, showed favor to your land;
    you restored the fortunes of Jacob.
2 You forgave the iniquity of your people
    and covered all their sins.
3 You set aside all your wrath
    and turned from your fierce anger.

4 Restore us again, God our Savior,
    and put away your displeasure toward us.
5 Will you be angry with us forever?
    Will you prolong your anger through all
      generations?
6 Will you not revive us again,
    that your people may rejoice in you?
7 Show us your unfailing love, LORD,
    and grant us your salvation.

8 I will listen to what God the LORD says;
    he promises peace to his people, his faithful
      servants —
    but let them not turn to folly.
9 Surely his salvation is near those who fear
      him,
    that his glory may dwell in our land.

10 Love and faithfulness meet together;
    righteousness and peace kiss each other.

11   Faithfulness springs forth from the earth,
        and righteousness looks down from heaven.
12   The Lord will indeed give what is good,
        and our land will yield its harvest.
13   Righteousness goes before him
        and prepares the way for his steps.

PSALM 86

A prayer of David.

1   Hear me, LORD, and answer me,
       for I am poor and needy.
2   Guard my life, for I am faithful to you;
       save your servant who trusts in you.
    You are my God;
3   have mercy on me, Lord,
       for I call to you all day long.
4   Bring joy to your servant, Lord,
       for I put my trust in you.

5   You, Lord, are forgiving and good,
       abounding in love to all who call to you.
6   Hear my prayer, LORD;
       listen to my cry for mercy.
7   When I am in distress, I call to you,
       because you answer me.

8   Among the gods there is none like you, Lord;
       no deeds can compare with yours.
9   All the nations you have made
       will come and worship before you, Lord;
       they will bring glory to your name.
10 For you are great and do marvelous deeds;
       you alone are God.

11 Teach me your way, LORD,
       that I may rely on your faithfulness;

give me an undivided heart,
that I may fear your name.

12 I will praise you, Lord my God, with all my
heart;
I will glorify your name forever.

13 For great is your love toward me;
you have delivered me from the depths,
from the realm of the dead.

14 Arrogant foes are attacking me, O God;
ruthless people are trying to kill me —
they have no regard for you.

15 But you, Lord, are a compassionate and
gracious God,
slow to anger, abounding in love and
faithfulness.

16 Turn to me and have mercy on me;
show your strength in behalf of your
servant;
save me, because I serve you
just as my mother did.

17 Give me a sign of your goodness,
that my enemies may see it and be put to
shame,
for you, LORD, have helped me and
comforted me.

PSALM 87

Of the Sons of Korah. A psalm. A song.

1   He has founded his city on the holy mountain.
2   The L ORD loves the gates of Zion
         more than all the other dwellings of Jacob.

3   Glorious things are said of you,
         city of God:
4   "I will record Rahab and Babylon
         among those who acknowledge me —
    Philistia too, and Tyre, along with Cush —
         and will say, 'This one was born in Zion.'"
5   Indeed, of Zion it will be said,
         "This one and that one were born in her,
         and the Most High himself will establish
            her."
6   The L ORD will write in the register of the
            peoples:
         "This one was born in Zion."

7   As they make music they will sing,
         "All my fountains are in you."

PSALM 88

A song. A psalm of the Sons of Korah. For the director of music. According to mahalath leannoth. *A maskil of Heman the Ezrahite.*

1 LORD, you are the God who saves me;
    day and night I cry out to you.
2 May my prayer come before you;
    turn your ear to my cry.

3 I am overwhelmed with troubles
    and my life draws near to death.
4 I am counted among those who go down to
        the pit;
    I am like one without strength.
5 I am set apart with the dead,
    like the slain who lie in the grave,
  whom you remember no more,
    who are cut off from your care.

6 You have put me in the lowest pit,
    in the darkest depths.
7 Your wrath lies heavily on me;
    you have overwhelmed me with all your
        waves.
8 You have taken from me my closest
        friends
    and have made me repulsive to them.
  I am confined and cannot escape;
9   my eyes are dim with grief.

I call to you, LORD, every day;
 I spread out my hands to you.
10 Do you show your wonders to the dead?
 Do their spirits rise up and praise you?
11 Is your love declared in the grave,
 your faithfulness in Destruction?
12 Are your wonders known in the place of
  darkness,
 or your righteous deeds in the land of
  oblivion?

13 But I cry to you for help, LORD;
 in the morning my prayer comes before you.
14 Why, LORD, do you reject me
 and hide your face from me?

15 From my youth I have suffered and been close
  to death;
 I have borne your terrors and am in despair.
16 Your wrath has swept over me;
 your terrors have destroyed me.
17 All day long they surround me like a flood;
 they have completely engulfed me.
18 You have taken from me friend and
  neighbor—
 darkness is my closest friend.

PSALM 89

A maskil *of Ethan the Ezrahite.*

1 I will sing of the LORD's great love forever;
    with my mouth I will make your faithfulness
        known
    through all generations.
2 I will declare that your love stands firm
        forever,
    that you have established your faithfulness
        in heaven itself.
3 You said, "I have made a covenant with my
        chosen one,
    I have sworn to David my servant,
4 'I will establish your line forever
    and make your throne firm through all
        generations.'"

5 The heavens praise your wonders, LORD,
    your faithfulness too, in the assembly of the
        holy ones.
6 For who in the skies above can compare with
        the LORD?
    Who is like the LORD among the heavenly
        beings?
7 In the council of the holy ones God is greatly
        feared;
    he is more awesome than all who surround
        him.

8 Who is like you, LORD God Almighty?
      You, LORD, are mighty, and your faithfulness
         surrounds you.

9 You rule over the surging sea;
      when its waves mount up, you still them.
10 You crushed Rahab like one of the slain;
      with your strong arm you scattered your
         enemies.
11 The heavens are yours, and yours also the
         earth;
      you founded the world and all that is in it.
12 You created the north and the south;
      Tabor and Hermon sing for joy at your
         name.
13 Your arm is endowed with power;
      your hand is strong, your right hand
         exalted.

14 Righteousness and justice are the foundation
         of your throne;
      love and faithfulness go before you.
15 Blessed are those who have learned to acclaim
         you,
      who walk in the light of your presence,
         LORD.
16 They rejoice in your name all day long;
      they celebrate your righteousness.
17 For you are their glory and strength,
      and by your favor you exalt our horn.
18 Indeed, our shield belongs to the LORD,
      our king to the Holy One of Israel.

19 Once you spoke in a vision,
       to your faithful people you said:
   "I have bestowed strength on a warrior;
       I have raised up a young man from among
           the people.
20 I have found David my servant;
       with my sacred oil I have anointed him.
21 My hand will sustain him;
       surely my arm will strengthen him.
22 The enemy will not get the better of him;
       the wicked will not oppress him.
23 I will crush his foes before him
       and strike down his adversaries.
24 My faithful love will be with him,
       and through my name his horn will be
           exalted.
25 I will set his hand over the sea,
       his right hand over the rivers.
26 He will call out to me, 'You are my Father,
       my God, the Rock my Savior.'
27 And I will appoint him to be my firstborn,
       the most exalted of the kings of the
           earth.
28 I will maintain my love to him forever,
       and my covenant with him will never fail.
29 I will establish his line forever,
       his throne as long as the heavens endure.

30 "If his sons forsake my law
       and do not follow my statutes,
31 if they violate my decrees
       and fail to keep my commands,

32 I will punish their sin with the rod,
their iniquity with flogging;
33 but I will not take my love from him,
nor will I ever betray my faithfulness.
34 I will not violate my covenant
or alter what my lips have uttered.
35 Once for all, I have sworn by my holiness —
and I will not lie to David —
36 that his line will continue forever
and his throne endure before me like
the sun;
37 it will be established forever like the
moon,
the faithful witness in the sky."

38 But you have rejected, you have spurned,
you have been very angry with your
anointed one.
39 You have renounced the covenant with your
servant
and have defiled his crown in the dust.
40 You have broken through all his walls
and reduced his strongholds to ruins.
41 All who pass by have plundered him;
he has become the scorn of his neighbors.
42 You have exalted the right hand of his foes;
you have made all his enemies rejoice.
43 Indeed, you have turned back the edge of his
sword
and have not supported him in battle.
44 You have put an end to his splendor
and cast his throne to the ground.

45   You have cut short the days of his youth;
           you have covered him with a mantle of
                shame.

46   How long, LORD? Will you hide yourself
                forever?
           How long will your wrath burn like fire?
47   Remember how fleeting is my life.
           For what futility you have created all
                humanity!
48   Who can live and not see death,
           or who can escape the power of the grave?
49   Lord, where is your former great love,
           which in your faithfulness you swore to
                David?
50   Remember, Lord, how your servant has been
                mocked,
           how I bear in my heart the taunts of all the
                nations,
51   the taunts with which your enemies, LORD,
                have mocked,
           with which they have mocked every step of
                your anointed one.

52   Praise be to the LORD forever!
           Amen and Amen.

BOOK IV

Psalms 90 – 106

PSALM 90

A prayer of Moses the man of God.

1   Lord, you have been our dwelling place
      throughout all generations.
2   Before the mountains were born
      or you brought forth the whole world,
      from everlasting to everlasting you
         are God.

3   You turn people back to dust,
      saying, "Return to dust, you mortals."
4   A thousand years in your sight
      are like a day that has just gone by,
      or like a watch in the night.
5   Yet you sweep people away in the sleep of
         death —
      they are like the new grass of the morning:
6   In the morning it springs up new,
      but by evening it is dry and withered.

7   We are consumed by your anger
      and terrified by your indignation.
8   You have set our iniquities before you,
      our secret sins in the light of your
         presence.
9   All our days pass away under your wrath;
      we finish our years with a moan.
10 Our days may come to seventy years,
      or eighty, if our strength endures;

yet the best of them are but trouble and
      sorrow,
    for they quickly pass, and we fly away.
11   If only we knew the power of your anger!
      Your wrath is as great as the fear that is your
         due.
12   Teach us to number our days,
      that we may gain a heart of wisdom.

13   Relent, LORD! How long will it be?
      Have compassion on your servants.
14   Satisfy us in the morning with your unfailing
      love,
      that we may sing for joy and be glad all our
         days.
15   Make us glad for as many days as you have
      afflicted us,
      for as many years as we have seen trouble.
16   May your deeds be shown to your servants,
      your splendor to their children.

17   May the favor of the Lord our God rest on us;
      establish the work of our hands for us —
      yes, establish the work of our hands.

PSALM 91

1   Whoever dwells in the shelter of the
        Most High
      will rest in the shadow of the Almighty.
2   I will say of the LORD, "He is my refuge and
        my fortress,
      my God, in whom I trust."

3   Surely he will save you
      from the fowler's snare
      and from the deadly pestilence.
4   He will cover you with his feathers,
      and under his wings you will find refuge;
      his faithfulness will be your shield and
        rampart.
5   You will not fear the terror of night,
      nor the arrow that flies by day,
6   nor the pestilence that stalks in the darkness,
      nor the plague that destroys at midday.
7   A thousand may fall at your side,
      ten thousand at your right hand,
      but it will not come near you.
8   You will only observe with your eyes
      and see the punishment of the wicked.

9   If you say, "The LORD is my refuge,"
      and you make the Most High your dwelling,
10 no harm will overtake you,
      no disaster will come near your tent.

11 For he will command his angels concerning
    you
      to guard you in all your ways;
12 they will lift you up in their hands,
      so that you will not strike your foot against a
      stone.
13 You will tread on the lion and the cobra;
      you will trample the great lion and the
      serpent.

14 "Because he loves me," says the LORD, "I will
      rescue him;
      I will protect him, for he acknowledges my
      name.
15 He will call on me, and I will answer him;
      I will be with him in trouble,
      I will deliver him and honor him.
16 With long life I will satisfy him
      and show him my salvation."

PSALM 92

A psalm. A song. For the Sabbath day.

1 It is good to praise the LORD
     and make music to your name,
       O Most High,
2 proclaiming your love in the morning
     and your faithfulness at night,
3 to the music of the ten-stringed lyre
     and the melody of the harp.

4 For you make me glad by your deeds, LORD;
     I sing for joy at what your hands have
       done.
5 How great are your works, LORD,
     how profound your thoughts!
6 Senseless people do not know,
     fools do not understand,
7 that though the wicked spring up like grass
     and all evildoers flourish,
      they will be destroyed forever.

8 But you, LORD, are forever exalted.

9 For surely your enemies, LORD,
     surely your enemies will perish;
     all evildoers will be scattered.
10 You have exalted my horn like that of a
     wild ox;
     fine oils have been poured on me.

11   My eyes have seen the defeat of my
          adversaries;
       my ears have heard the rout of my wicked
          foes.

12   The righteous will flourish like a palm tree,
          they will grow like a cedar of Lebanon;
13   planted in the house of the LORD,
          they will flourish in the courts of our God.
14   They will still bear fruit in old age,
          they will stay fresh and green,
15   proclaiming, "The LORD is upright;
          he is my Rock, and there is no wickedness
          in him."

PSALM 93

1   The Lord reigns, he is robed in majesty;
    the Lord is robed in majesty and armed
      with strength;
    indeed, the world is established, firm and
      secure.
2   Your throne was established long ago;
    you are from all eternity.

3   The seas have lifted up, Lord,
    the seas have lifted up their voice;
    the seas have lifted up their pounding
      waves.
4   Mightier than the thunder of the great waters,
    mightier than the breakers of the sea —
    the Lord on high is mighty.

5   Your statutes, Lord, stand firm;
    holiness adorns your house
    for endless days.

PSALM 94

1 The LORD is a God who avenges.
    O God who avenges, shine forth.
2 Rise up, Judge of the earth;
    pay back to the proud what they deserve.
3 How long, LORD, will the wicked,
    how long will the wicked be jubilant?

4 They pour out arrogant words;
    all the evildoers are full of boasting.
5 They crush your people, LORD;
    they oppress your inheritance.
6 They slay the widow and the foreigner;
    they murder the fatherless.
7 They say, "The LORD does not see;
    the God of Jacob takes no notice."

8 Take notice, you senseless ones among the people;
    you fools, when will you become wise?
9 Does he who fashioned the ear not hear?
    Does he who formed the eye not see?
10 Does he who disciplines nations not punish?
    Does he who teaches mankind lack knowledge?
11 The LORD knows all human plans;
    he knows that they are futile.

12 Blessed is the one you discipline, LORD,
    the one you teach from your law;

13 you grant them relief from days of trouble,
        till a pit is dug for the wicked.
14 For the LORD will not reject his people;
        he will never forsake his inheritance.
15 Judgment will again be founded on
            righteousness,
        and all the upright in heart will follow it.

16 Who will rise up for me against the wicked?
        Who will take a stand for me against
            evildoers?
17 Unless the LORD had given me help,
        I would soon have dwelt in the silence of
            death.
18 When I said, "My foot is slipping,"
        your unfailing love, LORD, supported me.
19 When anxiety was great within me,
        your consolation brought me joy.

20 Can a corrupt throne be allied with you —
        a throne that brings on misery by its
            decrees?
21 The wicked band together against the
            righteous
        and condemn the innocent to death.
22 But the LORD has become my fortress,
        and my God the rock in whom I take refuge.
23 He will repay them for their sins
        and destroy them for their wickedness;
        the LORD our God will destroy them.

PSALM 95

1   Come, let us sing for joy to the Lord;
      let us shout aloud to the Rock of our
         salvation.
2   Let us come before him with thanksgiving
      and extol him with music and song.

3   For the Lord is the great God,
      the great King above all gods.
4   In his hand are the depths of the earth,
      and the mountain peaks belong to
         him.
5   The sea is his, for he made it,
      and his hands formed the dry land.

6   Come, let us bow down in worship,
      let us kneel before the Lord our Maker;
7   for he is our God
      and we are the people of his pasture,
      the flock under his care.

      Today, if only you would hear his voice,
8   "Do not harden your hearts as you did at
         Meribah,
      as you did that day at Massah in the
         wilderness,
9   where your ancestors tested me;
      they tried me, though they had seen what
         I did.

10   For forty years I was angry with that
              generation;
          I said, 'They are a people whose hearts go
              astray,
          and they have not known my ways.'
11   So I declared on oath in my anger,
          'They shall never enter my rest.' "

PSALM 96

1   Sing to the LORD a new song;
        sing to the LORD, all the earth.
2   Sing to the LORD, praise his name;
        proclaim his salvation day after day.
3   Declare his glory among the nations,
        his marvelous deeds among all peoples.

4   For great is the LORD and most worthy of
            praise;
        he is to be feared above all gods.
5   For all the gods of the nations are idols,
        but the LORD made the heavens.
6   Splendor and majesty are before him;
        strength and glory are in his sanctuary.

7   Ascribe to the LORD, all you families of
            nations,
        ascribe to the LORD glory and strength.
8   Ascribe to the LORD the glory due his name;
        bring an offering and come into his
            courts.
9   Worship the LORD in the splendor of his
            holiness;
        tremble before him, all the earth.
10 Say among the nations, "The LORD reigns."
        The world is firmly established, it cannot
            be moved;
        he will judge the peoples with equity.

11   Let the heavens rejoice, let the earth be glad;
       let the sea resound, and all that is in it.
12   Let the fields be jubilant, and everything in
          them;
       let all the trees of the forest sing for joy.
13   Let all creation rejoice before the LORD, for he
          comes,
       he comes to judge the earth.
    He will judge the world in righteousness
       and the peoples in his faithfulness.

PSALM 97

1   The LORD reigns, let the earth be glad;
      let the distant shores rejoice.

2   Clouds and thick darkness surround him;
      righteousness and justice are the foundation
         of his throne.

3   Fire goes before him
      and consumes his foes on every side.

4   His lightning lights up the world;
      the earth sees and trembles.

5   The mountains melt like wax before the LORD,
      before the Lord of all the earth.

6   The heavens proclaim his righteousness,
      and all peoples see his glory.

7   All who worship images are put to shame,
      those who boast in idols —
    worship him, all you gods!

8   Zion hears and rejoices
      and the villages of Judah are glad
      because of your judgments, LORD.

9   For you, LORD, are the Most High over all the
         earth;
      you are exalted far above all gods.

10   Let those who love the LORD hate evil,
      for he guards the lives of his faithful ones
      and delivers them from the hand of the
         wicked.

11   Light shines on the righteous
         and joy on the upright in heart.
12   Rejoice in the LORD, you who are righteous,
         and praise his holy name.

PSALM 98

A psalm.

1   Sing to the LORD a new song,
     for he has done marvelous things;
  his right hand and his holy arm
     have worked salvation for him.

2   The LORD has made his salvation known
     and revealed his righteousness to the nations.

3   He has remembered his love
     and his faithfulness to Israel;
  all the ends of the earth have seen
     the salvation of our God.

4   Shout for joy to the LORD, all the earth,
     burst into jubilant song with music;

5   make music to the LORD with the harp,
     with the harp and the sound of singing,

6   with trumpets and the blast of the ram's
       horn—
     shout for joy before the LORD, the King.

7   Let the sea resound, and everything in it,
     the world, and all who live in it.

8   Let the rivers clap their hands,
     let the mountains sing together for joy;

9   let them sing before the LORD,
     for he comes to judge the earth.
  He will judge the world in righteousness
     and the peoples with equity.

PSALM 99

1 The LORD reigns,
    let the nations tremble;
he sits enthroned between the cherubim,
    let the earth shake.
2 Great is the LORD in Zion;
    he is exalted over all the nations.
3 Let them praise your great and awesome
        name —
    he is holy.

4 The King is mighty, he loves justice —
    you have established equity;
in Jacob you have done
    what is just and right.
5 Exalt the LORD our God
    and worship at his footstool;
    he is holy.

6 Moses and Aaron were among his
        priests,
    Samuel was among those who called
        on his name;
they called on the LORD
    and he answered them.
7 He spoke to them from the pillar of
        cloud;
    they kept his statutes and the decrees
        he gave them.

8   LORD our God,
         you answered them;
     you were to Israel a forgiving God,
         though you punished their misdeeds.
9   Exalt the LORD our God
         and worship at his holy mountain,
         for the LORD our God is holy.

PSALM 100

A psalm. For giving grateful praise.

1   Shout for joy to the Lord, all the earth.
2   Worship the Lord with gladness;
       come before him with joyful songs.
3   Know that the Lord is God.
       It is he who made us, and we are his;
       we are his people, the sheep of his pasture.

4   Enter his gates with thanksgiving
       and his courts with praise;
       give thanks to him and praise his name.
5   For the Lord is good and his love endures
       forever;
       his faithfulness continues through all
       generations.

PSALM 101

Of David. A psalm.

1   I will sing of your love and justice;
      to you, LORD, I will sing praise.

2   I will be careful to lead a blameless life —
      when will you come to me?

   I will conduct the affairs of my house
      with a blameless heart.

3   I will not look with approval
      on anything that is vile.

   I hate what faithless people do;
      I will have no part in it.

4   The perverse of heart shall be far
         from me;
      I will have nothing to do with what
         is evil.

5   Whoever slanders their neighbor in secret,
      I will put to silence;
   whoever has haughty eyes and a proud
         heart,
      I will not tolerate.

6   My eyes will be on the faithful in the
         land,
      that they may dwell with me;
   the one whose walk is blameless
      will minister to me.

7   No one who practices deceit
        will dwell in my house;
    no one who speaks falsely
        will stand in my presence.

8   Every morning I will put to silence
        all the wicked in the land;
    I will cut off every evildoer
        from the city of the LORD.

PSALM 102

A prayer of an afflicted person who has grown
weak and pours out a lament before the LORD.

1 Hear my prayer, LORD;
　　let my cry for help come to you.
2 Do not hide your face from me
　　when I am in distress.
　Turn your ear to me;
　　when I call, answer me quickly.

3 For my days vanish like smoke;
　　my bones burn like glowing embers.
4 My heart is blighted and withered like grass;
　　I forget to eat my food.
5 In my distress I groan aloud
　　and am reduced to skin and bones.
6 I am like a desert owl,
　　like an owl among the ruins.
7 I lie awake; I have become
　　like a bird alone on a roof.
8 All day long my enemies taunt me;
　　those who rail against me use my name as a
　　　　curse.
9 For I eat ashes as my food
　　and mingle my drink with tears
10 because of your great wrath,
　　for you have taken me up and thrown me
　　　　aside.

11 My days are like the evening shadow;
    I wither away like grass.

12 But you, LORD, sit enthroned forever;
    your renown endures through all
        generations.
13 You will arise and have compassion on Zion,
    for it is time to show favor to her;
    the appointed time has come.
14 For her stones are dear to your servants;
    her very dust moves them to pity.
15 The nations will fear the name of the LORD,
    all the kings of the earth will revere your
        glory.
16 For the LORD will rebuild Zion
    and appear in his glory.
17 He will respond to the prayer of the destitute;
    he will not despise their plea.

18 Let this be written for a future generation,
    that a people not yet created may praise the
        LORD:
19 "The LORD looked down from his sanctuary on
        high,
    from heaven he viewed the earth,
20 to hear the groans of the prisoners
    and release those condemned to death."
21 So the name of the LORD will be declared in
        Zion
    and his praise in Jerusalem
22 when the peoples and the kingdoms
    assemble to worship the LORD.

23 In the course of my life he broke my strength;
        he cut short my days.
24 So I said:
    "Do not take me away, my God, in the midst of
            my days;
        your years go on through all generations.
25 In the beginning you laid the foundations of
            the earth,
        and the heavens are the work of your hands.
26 They will perish, but you remain;
        they will all wear out like a garment.
    Like clothing you will change them
        and they will be discarded.
27 But you remain the same,
        and your years will never end.
28 The children of your servants will live in your
            presence;
        their descendants will be established before
            you."

PSALM 103

Of David.

1 Praise the LORD, my soul;
  all my inmost being, praise his holy name.
2 Praise the LORD, my soul,
  and forget not all his benefits —
3 who forgives all your sins
  and heals all your diseases,
4 who redeems your life from the pit
  and crowns you with love and compassion,
5 who satisfies your desires with good things
  so that your youth is renewed like the
    eagle's.

6 The LORD works righteousness
  and justice for all the oppressed.

7 He made known his ways to Moses,
  his deeds to the people of Israel:
8 The LORD is compassionate and gracious,
  slow to anger, abounding in love.
9 He will not always accuse,
  nor will he harbor his anger forever;
10 he does not treat us as our sins deserve
  or repay us according to our iniquities.
11 For as high as the heavens are above the
    earth,
  so great is his love for those who fear
    him;

12   as far as the east is from the west,
       so far has he removed our transgressions
          from us.

13   As a father has compassion on his children,
       so the Lord has compassion on those who
          fear him;
14   for he knows how we are formed,
       he remembers that we are dust.
15   The life of mortals is like grass,
       they flourish like a flower of the field;
16   the wind blows over it and it is gone,
       and its place remembers it no more.
17   But from everlasting to everlasting
       the Lord's love is with those who fear him,
       and his righteousness with their children's
          children —
18   with those who keep his covenant
       and remember to obey his precepts.

19   The Lord has established his throne in heaven,
       and his kingdom rules over all.

20   Praise the Lord, you his angels,
       you mighty ones who do his bidding,
       who obey his word.
21   Praise the Lord, all his heavenly hosts,
       you his servants who do his will.
22   Praise the Lord, all his works
       everywhere in his dominion.

     Praise the Lord, my soul.

PSALM 104

1   Praise the LORD, my soul.

LORD my God, you are very great;
    you are clothed with splendor and
       majesty.

2   The LORD wraps himself in light as with a
       garment;
    he stretches out the heavens like a tent
3   and lays the beams of his upper chambers
       on their waters.
He makes the clouds his chariot
    and rides on the wings of the wind.
4   He makes winds his messengers,
    flames of fire his servants.

5   He set the earth on its foundations;
    it can never be moved.
6   You covered it with the watery depths as
       with a garment;
    the waters stood above the mountains.
7   But at your rebuke the waters fled,
    at the sound of your thunder they took to
       flight;
8   they flowed over the mountains,
    they went down into the valleys,
    to the place you assigned for them.
9   You set a boundary they cannot cross;
    never again will they cover the earth.

10   He makes springs pour water into the ravines;
         it flows between the mountains.
11   They give water to all the beasts of the field;
         the wild donkeys quench their thirst.
12   The birds of the sky nest by the waters;
         they sing among the branches.
13   He waters the mountains from his upper
                chambers;
         the land is satisfied by the fruit of his work.
14   He makes grass grow for the cattle,
         and plants for people to cultivate —
         bringing forth food from the earth:
15   wine that gladdens human hearts,
         oil to make their faces shine,
         and bread that sustains their hearts.
16   The trees of the LORD are well watered,
         the cedars of Lebanon that he planted.
17   There the birds make their nests;
         the stork has its home in the junipers.
18   The high mountains belong to the wild goats;
         the crags are a refuge for the hyrax.

19   He made the moon to mark the seasons,
         and the sun knows when to go down.
20   You bring darkness, it becomes night,
         and all the beasts of the forest prowl.
21   The lions roar for their prey
         and seek their food from God.
22   The sun rises, and they steal away;
         they return and lie down in their dens.
23   Then people go out to their work,
         to their labor until evening.

24 How many are your works, LORD!
    In wisdom you made them all;
    the earth is full of your creatures.
25 There is the sea, vast and spacious,
    teeming with creatures beyond number —
    living things both large and small.
26 There the ships go to and fro,
    and Leviathan, which you formed to frolic
        there.

27 All creatures look to you
    to give them their food at the proper
        time.
28 When you give it to them,
    they gather it up;
when you open your hand,
    they are satisfied with good things.
29 When you hide your face,
    they are terrified;
when you take away their breath,
    they die and return to the dust.
30 When you send your Spirit,
    they are created,
    and you renew the face of the ground.

31 May the glory of the LORD endure forever;
    may the LORD rejoice in his works —
32 he who looks at the earth, and it trembles,
    who touches the mountains, and they
        smoke.

33 I will sing to the LORD all my life;
    I will sing praise to my God as long as I live.

34   May my meditation be pleasing to him,
        as I rejoice in the LORD.
35   But may sinners vanish from the earth
        and the wicked be no more.

Praise the LORD, my soul.

Praise the LORD.

PSALM 105

1   Give praise to the L<small>ORD</small>, proclaim his name;
    make known among the nations what he
        has done.
2   Sing to him, sing praise to him;
    tell of all his wonderful acts.
3   Glory in his holy name;
    let the hearts of those who seek the L<small>ORD</small>
        rejoice.
4   Look to the L<small>ORD</small> and his strength;
    seek his face always.

5   Remember the wonders he has done,
    his miracles, and the judgments he
        pronounced,
6   you his servants, the descendants of Abraham,
    his chosen ones, the children of Jacob.
7   He is the L<small>ORD</small> our God;
    his judgments are in all the earth.

8   He remembers his covenant forever,
    the promise he made, for a thousand
        generations,
9   the covenant he made with Abraham,
    the oath he swore to Isaac.
10   He confirmed it to Jacob as a decree,
    to Israel as an everlasting covenant:
11   "To you I will give the land of Canaan
    as the portion you will inherit."

12 When they were but few in number,
   few indeed, and strangers in it,
13 they wandered from nation to nation,
   from one kingdom to another.
14 He allowed no one to oppress them;
   for their sake he rebuked kings:
15 "Do not touch my anointed ones;
   do my prophets no harm."

16 He called down famine on the land
   and destroyed all their supplies of food;
17 and he sent a man before them —
   Joseph, sold as a slave.
18 They bruised his feet with shackles,
   his neck was put in irons,
19 till what he foretold came to pass,
   till the word of the LORD proved him
      true.
20 The king sent and released him,
   the ruler of peoples set him free.
21 He made him master of his household,
   ruler over all he possessed,
22 to instruct his princes as he pleased
   and teach his elders wisdom.

23 Then Israel entered Egypt;
   Jacob resided as a foreigner in the land of
      Ham.
24 The LORD made his people very fruitful;
   he made them too numerous for their foes,
25 whose hearts he turned to hate his people,
   to conspire against his servants.

26 He sent Moses his servant,
   and Aaron, whom he had chosen.
27 They performed his signs among them,
   his wonders in the land of Ham.
28 He sent darkness and made the land dark —
   for had they not rebelled against his words?
29 He turned their waters into blood,
   causing their fish to die.
30 Their land teemed with frogs,
   which went up into the bedrooms of their
      rulers.
31 He spoke, and there came swarms of flies,
   and gnats throughout their country.
32 He turned their rain into hail,
   with lightning throughout their land;
33 he struck down their vines and fig trees
   and shattered the trees of their country.
34 He spoke, and the locusts came,
   grasshoppers without number;
35 they ate up every green thing in their land,
   ate up the produce of their soil.
36 Then he struck down all the firstborn in their
      land,
   the firstfruits of all their manhood.
37 He brought out Israel, laden with silver and
      gold,
   and from among their tribes no one faltered.
38 Egypt was glad when they left,
   because dread of Israel had fallen on them.

39 He spread out a cloud as a covering,
   and a fire to give light at night.

40   They asked, and he brought them quail;
        he fed them well with the bread of heaven.
41   He opened the rock, and water gushed out;
        it flowed like a river in the desert.

42   For he remembered his holy promise
        given to his servant Abraham.
43   He brought out his people with rejoicing,
        his chosen ones with shouts of joy;
44   he gave them the lands of the nations,
        and they fell heir to what others had toiled
            for —
45   that they might keep his precepts
        and observe his laws.

Praise the LORD.

PSALM 106

1 Praise the LORD.

Give thanks to the LORD, for he is good;
   his love endures forever.

2 Who can proclaim the mighty acts of the LORD
   or fully declare his praise?
3 Blessed are those who act justly,
   who always do what is right.

4 Remember me, LORD, when you show favor to
      your people,
   come to my aid when you save them,
5 that I may enjoy the prosperity of your chosen
      ones,
   that I may share in the joy of your nation
   and join your inheritance in giving praise.

6 We have sinned, even as our ancestors did;
   we have done wrong and acted wickedly.
7 When our ancestors were in Egypt,
   they gave no thought to your miracles;
   they did not remember your many kindnesses,
   and they rebelled by the sea, the Red Sea.
8 Yet he saved them for his name's sake,
   to make his mighty power known.
9 He rebuked the Red Sea, and it dried up;
   he led them through the depths as through a
      desert.

10 He saved them from the hand of the foe;
        from the hand of the enemy he redeemed
            them.
11 The waters covered their adversaries;
        not one of them survived.
12 Then they believed his promises
        and sang his praise.

13 But they soon forgot what he had done
        and did not wait for his plan to unfold.
14 In the desert they gave in to their craving;
        in the wilderness they put God to the
            test.
15 So he gave them what they asked for,
        but sent a wasting disease among them.

16 In the camp they grew envious of Moses
        and of Aaron, who was consecrated to
            the LORD.
17 The earth opened up and swallowed
            Dathan;
        it buried the company of Abiram.
18 Fire blazed among their followers;
        a flame consumed the wicked.
19 At Horeb they made a calf
        and worshiped an idol cast from metal.
20 They exchanged their glorious God
        for an image of a bull, which eats grass.
21 They forgot the God who saved them,
        who had done great things in Egypt,
22 miracles in the land of Ham
        and awesome deeds by the Red Sea.

23 So he said he would destroy them —
    had not Moses, his chosen one,
stood in the breach before him
    to keep his wrath from destroying them.

24 Then they despised the pleasant land;
    they did not believe his promise.
25 They grumbled in their tents
    and did not obey the LORD.
26 So he swore to them with uplifted hand
    that he would make them fall in the
        wilderness,
27 make their descendants fall among the
        nations
    and scatter them throughout the lands.

28 They yoked themselves to the Baal of Peor
    and ate sacrifices offered to lifeless gods;
29 they aroused the LORD's anger by their
        wicked deeds,
    and a plague broke out among them.
30 But Phinehas stood up and intervened,
    and the plague was checked.
31 This was credited to him as righteousness
    for endless generations to come.
32 By the waters of Meribah they angered the
        LORD,
    and trouble came to Moses because of
        them;
33 for they rebelled against the Spirit of
        God,
    and rash words came from Moses' lips.

34 They did not destroy the peoples
    as the Lord had commanded them,
35 but they mingled with the nations
    and adopted their customs.
36 They worshiped their idols,
    which became a snare to them.
37 They sacrificed their sons
    and their daughters to false gods.
38 They shed innocent blood,
    the blood of their sons and daughters,
whom they sacrificed to the idols of Canaan,
    and the land was desecrated by their
        blood.
39 They defiled themselves by what they did;
    by their deeds they prostituted themselves.

40 Therefore the Lord was angry with his
        people
    and abhorred his inheritance.
41 He gave them into the hands of the nations,
    and their foes ruled over them.
42 Their enemies oppressed them
    and subjected them to their power.
43 Many times he delivered them,
    but they were bent on rebellion
    and they wasted away in their sin.
44 Yet he took note of their distress
    when he heard their cry;
45 for their sake he remembered his covenant
    and out of his great love he relented.
46 He caused all who held them captive
    to show them mercy.

47   Save us, LORD our God,
        and gather us from the nations,
    that we may give thanks to your holy name
        and glory in your praise.

48   Praise be to the LORD, the God of Israel,
        from everlasting to everlasting.

Let all the people say, "Amen!"

Praise the LORD.

BOOK V

Psalms 107–150

PSALM 107

1   Give thanks to the LORD, for he is good;
        his love endures forever.

2   Let the redeemed of the LORD tell their story—
        those he redeemed from the hand of
            the foe,
3   those he gathered from the lands,
        from east and west, from north and south.

4   Some wandered in desert wastelands,
        finding no way to a city where they could
            settle.
5   They were hungry and thirsty,
        and their lives ebbed away.
6   Then they cried out to the LORD in their
            trouble,
        and he delivered them from their distress.
7   He led them by a straight way
        to a city where they could settle.
8   Let them give thanks to the LORD for his
            unfailing love
        and his wonderful deeds for mankind,
9   for he satisfies the thirsty
        and fills the hungry with good things.

10   Some sat in darkness, in utter darkness,
        prisoners suffering in iron chains,
11   because they rebelled against God's commands
        and despised the plans of the Most High.

12 So he subjected them to bitter labor;
    they stumbled, and there was no one to help.
13 Then they cried to the LORD in their trouble,
    and he saved them from their distress.
14 He brought them out of darkness, the utter
    darkness,
    and broke away their chains.
15 Let them give thanks to the LORD for his
    unfailing love
    and his wonderful deeds for mankind,
16 for he breaks down gates of bronze
    and cuts through bars of iron.

17 Some became fools through their rebellious
    ways
    and suffered affliction because of their
    iniquities.
18 They loathed all food
    and drew near the gates of death.
19 Then they cried to the LORD in their trouble,
    and he saved them from their distress.
20 He sent out his word and healed them;
    he rescued them from the grave.
21 Let them give thanks to the LORD for his
    unfailing love
    and his wonderful deeds for mankind.
22 Let them sacrifice thank offerings
    and tell of his works with songs of joy.

23 Some went out on the sea in ships;
    they were merchants on the mighty
    waters.

24 They saw the works of the L ORD,
   his wonderful deeds in the deep.
25 For he spoke and stirred up a tempest
   that lifted high the waves.
26 They mounted up to the heavens and went
      down to the depths;
   in their peril their courage melted away.
27 They reeled and staggered like drunkards;
   they were at their wits' end.
28 Then they cried out to the L ORD in their
      trouble,
   and he brought them out of their distress.
29 He stilled the storm to a whisper;
   the waves of the sea were hushed.
30 They were glad when it grew calm,
   and he guided them to their desired
      haven.
31 Let them give thanks to the L ORD for his
      unfailing love
   and his wonderful deeds for mankind.
32 Let them exalt him in the assembly of the
      people
   and praise him in the council of the elders.

33 He turned rivers into a desert,
   flowing springs into thirsty ground,
34 and fruitful land into a salt waste,
   because of the wickedness of those who
      lived there.
35 He turned the desert into pools of water
   and the parched ground into flowing
      springs;

36   there he brought the hungry to live,
       and they founded a city where they could
         settle.
37   They sowed fields and planted vineyards
       that yielded a fruitful harvest;
38   he blessed them, and their numbers greatly
         increased,
       and he did not let their herds diminish.

39   Then their numbers decreased, and they were
         humbled
       by oppression, calamity and sorrow;
40   he who pours contempt on nobles
       made them wander in a trackless waste.
41   But he lifted the needy out of their affliction
       and increased their families like flocks.
42   The upright see and rejoice,
       but all the wicked shut their mouths.

43   Let the one who is wise heed these things
       and ponder the loving deeds of the LORD.

PSALM 108

A song. A psalm of David.

1   My heart, O God, is steadfast;
     I will sing and make music with all my soul.
2   Awake, harp and lyre!
     I will awaken the dawn.
3   I will praise you, Lord, among the nations;
     I will sing of you among the peoples.
4   For great is your love, higher than the heavens;
     your faithfulness reaches to the skies.
5   Be exalted, O God, above the heavens;
     let your glory be over all the earth.

6   Save us and help us with your right hand,
     that those you love may be delivered.
7   God has spoken from his sanctuary:
     "In triumph I will parcel out Shechem
     and measure off the Valley of Sukkoth.
8   Gilead is mine, Manasseh is mine;
     Ephraim is my helmet,
     Judah is my scepter.
9   Moab is my washbasin,
     on Edom I toss my sandal;
     over Philistia I shout in triumph."

10   Who will bring me to the fortified city?
     Who will lead me to Edom?
11   Is it not you, God, you who have rejected us
     and no longer go out with our armies?

12   Give us aid against the enemy,
            for human help is worthless.
13   With God we will gain the victory,
            and he will trample down our enemies.

PSALM 109

For the director of music. Of David. A psalm.

1 My God, whom I praise,
    do not remain silent,
2 for people who are wicked and deceitful
    have opened their mouths against me;
    they have spoken against me with lying
        tongues.
3 With words of hatred they surround me;
    they attack me without cause.
4 In return for my friendship they accuse me,
    but I am a man of prayer.
5 They repay me evil for good,
    and hatred for my friendship.

6 Appoint someone evil to oppose my enemy;
    let an accuser stand at his right hand.
7 When he is tried, let him be found guilty,
    and may his prayers condemn him.
8 May his days be few;
    may another take his place of leadership.
9 May his children be fatherless
    and his wife a widow.
10 May his children be wandering beggars;
    may they be driven from their ruined
        homes.
11 May a creditor seize all he has;
    may strangers plunder the fruits of his labor.

12   May no one extend kindness to him
        or take pity on his fatherless children.
13   May his descendants be cut off,
        their names blotted out from the next
            generation.
14   May the iniquity of his fathers be remembered
            before the LORD;
        may the sin of his mother never be blotted
            out.
15   May their sins always remain before the LORD,
        that he may blot out their name from the
            earth.

16   For he never thought of doing a kindness,
        but hounded to death the poor
        and the needy and the brokenhearted.
17   He loved to pronounce a curse —
        may it come back on him.
     He found no pleasure in blessing —
        may it be far from him.
18   He wore cursing as his garment;
        it entered into his body like water,
        into his bones like oil.
19   May it be like a cloak wrapped about him,
        like a belt tied forever around him.
20   May this be the LORD's payment to my
            accusers,
        to those who speak evil of me.

21   But you, Sovereign LORD,
        help me for your name's sake;
        out of the goodness of your love, deliver me.

22   For I am poor and needy,
         and my heart is wounded within me.
23   I fade away like an evening shadow;
         I am shaken off like a locust.
24   My knees give way from fasting;
         my body is thin and gaunt.
25   I am an object of scorn to my accusers;
         when they see me, they shake their heads.

26   Help me, LORD my God;
         save me according to your unfailing love.
27   Let them know that it is your hand,
         that you, LORD, have done it.
28   While they curse, may you bless;
         may those who attack me be put to shame,
         but may your servant rejoice.
29   May my accusers be clothed with disgrace
         and wrapped in shame as in a cloak.

30   With my mouth I will greatly extol the LORD;
         in the great throng of worshipers I will
             praise him.
31   For he stands at the right hand of the needy,
         to save their lives from those who would
             condemn them.

PSALM 110

Of David. A psalm.

1 The LORD says to my lord:

"Sit at my right hand
until I make your enemies
a footstool for your feet."

2 The LORD will extend your mighty scepter from
Zion, saying,
"Rule in the midst of your enemies!"

3 Your troops will be willing
on your day of battle.
Arrayed in holy splendor,
your young men will come to you
like dew from the morning's womb.

4 The LORD has sworn
and will not change his mind:
"You are a priest forever,
in the order of Melchizedek."

5 The Lord is at your right hand;
he will crush kings on the day of his wrath.

6 He will judge the nations, heaping up the
dead
and crushing the rulers of the whole earth.

7 He will drink from a brook along the way,
and so he will lift his head high.

PSALM 111

1 Praise the LORD.

  I will extol the LORD with all my heart
    in the council of the upright and in the
      assembly.

2 Great are the works of the LORD;
    they are pondered by all who delight
      in them.
3 Glorious and majestic are his deeds,
    and his righteousness endures forever.
4 He has caused his wonders to be
      remembered;
    the LORD is gracious and compassionate.
5 He provides food for those who fear him;
    he remembers his covenant forever.

6 He has shown his people the power of his
      works,
    giving them the lands of other nations.
7 The works of his hands are faithful and
      just;
    all his precepts are trustworthy.
8 They are established for ever and ever,
    enacted in faithfulness and uprightness.
9 He provided redemption for his people;
    he ordained his covenant forever —
      holy and awesome is his name.

10   The fear of the Lord is the beginning of
                wisdom;
         all who follow his precepts have good
                understanding.
         To him belongs eternal praise.

PSALM 112

1   Praise the LORD.

    Blessed are those who fear the LORD,
        who find great delight in his commands.

2   Their children will be mighty in the land;
        the generation of the upright will be
            blessed.
3   Wealth and riches are in their houses,
        and their righteousness endures forever.
4   Even in darkness light dawns for the upright,
        for those who are gracious and
            compassionate and righteous.
5   Good will come to those who are generous and
            lend freely,
        who conduct their affairs with justice.

6   Surely the righteous will never be shaken;
        they will be remembered forever.
7   They will have no fear of bad news;
        their hearts are steadfast, trusting in the
            LORD.
8   Their hearts are secure, they will have no fear;
        in the end they will look in triumph on their
            foes.
9   They have freely scattered their gifts to the
            poor,
        their righteousness endures forever;
        their horn will be lifted high in honor.

10   The wicked will see and be vexed,
         they will gnash their teeth and waste away;
         the longings of the wicked will come to
             nothing.

PSALM 113

1   Praise the LORD.

     Praise the LORD, you his servants;
       praise the name of the LORD.

2   Let the name of the LORD be praised,
       both now and forevermore.

3   From the rising of the sun to the place where it
       sets,
       the name of the LORD is to be praised.

4   The LORD is exalted over all the nations,
       his glory above the heavens.

5   Who is like the LORD our God,
       the One who sits enthroned on high,

6   who stoops down to look
       on the heavens and the earth?

7   He raises the poor from the dust
       and lifts the needy from the ash heap;

8   he seats them with princes,
       with the princes of his people.

9   He settles the childless woman in her home
       as a happy mother of children.

     Praise the LORD.

PSALM 114

1   When Israel came out of Egypt,
      Jacob from a people of foreign tongue,
2   Judah became God's sanctuary,
      Israel his dominion.

3   The sea looked and fled,
      the Jordan turned back;
4   the mountains leaped like rams,
      the hills like lambs.

5   Why was it, sea, that you fled?
      Why, Jordan, did you turn back?
6   Why, mountains, did you leap like rams,
      you hills, like lambs?

7   Tremble, earth, at the presence of the Lord,
      at the presence of the God of Jacob,
8   who turned the rock into a pool,
      the hard rock into springs of water.

PSALM 115

1   Not to us, Lord, not to us
         but to your name be the glory,
         because of your love and faithfulness.

2   Why do the nations say,
         "Where is their God?"
3   Our God is in heaven;
         he does whatever pleases him.
4   But their idols are silver and gold,
         made by human hands.
5   They have mouths, but cannot speak,
         eyes, but cannot see.
6   They have ears, but cannot hear,
         noses, but cannot smell.
7   They have hands, but cannot feel,
         feet, but cannot walk,
         nor can they utter a sound with their
           throats.
8   Those who make them will be like
           them,
         and so will all who trust in them.

9   All you Israelites, trust in the Lord —
         he is their help and shield.
10   House of Aaron, trust in the Lord —
         he is their help and shield.
11   You who fear him, trust in the Lord —
         he is their help and shield.

12   The LORD remembers us and will bless us:
          He will bless his people Israel,
          he will bless the house of Aaron,
13   he will bless those who fear the LORD —
          small and great alike.

14   May the LORD cause you to flourish,
          both you and your children.
15   May you be blessed by the LORD,
          the Maker of heaven and earth.

16   The highest heavens belong to the LORD,
          but the earth he has given to mankind.
17   It is not the dead who praise the LORD,
          those who go down to the place of silence;
18   it is we who extol the LORD,
          both now and forevermore.

      Praise the LORD.

PSALM 116

1   I love the LORD, for he heard my voice;
        he heard my cry for mercy.
2   Because he turned his ear to me,
        I will call on him as long as I live.

3   The cords of death entangled me,
        the anguish of the grave came over me;
        I was overcome by distress and sorrow.
4   Then I called on the name of the LORD:
        "LORD, save me!"

5   The LORD is gracious and righteous;
        our God is full of compassion.
6   The LORD protects the unwary;
        when I was brought low, he saved me.

7   Return to your rest, my soul,
        for the LORD has been good to you.

8   For you, LORD, have delivered me from
                death,
        my eyes from tears,
        my feet from stumbling,
9   that I may walk before the LORD
        in the land of the living.

10 I trusted in the LORD when I said,
        "I am greatly afflicted";
11 in my alarm I said,
        "Everyone is a liar."

12   What shall I return to the LORD
        for all his goodness to me?

13   I will lift up the cup of salvation
        and call on the name of the LORD.
14   I will fulfill my vows to the LORD
        in the presence of all his people.

15   Precious in the sight of the LORD
        is the death of his faithful servants.
16   Truly I am your servant, LORD;
        I serve you just as my mother did;
        you have freed me from my chains.

17   I will sacrifice a thank offering to you
        and call on the name of the LORD.
18   I will fulfill my vows to the LORD
        in the presence of all his people,
19   in the courts of the house of the LORD —
        in your midst, Jerusalem.

     Praise the LORD.

PSALM 117

1   Praise the LORD, all you nations;
        extol him, all you peoples.
2   For great is his love toward us,
        and the faithfulness of the LORD endures
           forever.

Praise the LORD.

PSALM 118

1   Give thanks to the LORD, for he is good;
    his love endures forever.

2   Let Israel say:
    "His love endures forever."
3   Let the house of Aaron say:
    "His love endures forever."
4   Let those who fear the LORD say:
    "His love endures forever."

5   When hard pressed, I cried to the LORD;
    he brought me into a spacious place.
6   The LORD is with me; I will not be
    afraid.
    What can mere mortals do to me?
7   The LORD is with me; he is my helper.
    I look in triumph on my enemies.

8   It is better to take refuge in the LORD
    than to trust in humans.
9   It is better to take refuge in the LORD
    than to trust in princes.
10 All the nations surrounded me,
    but in the name of the LORD I cut them
    down.
11 They surrounded me on every side,
    but in the name of the LORD I cut them
    down.

12 They swarmed around me like bees,
      but they were consumed as quickly as
          burning thorns;
      in the name of the LORD I cut them down.
13 I was pushed back and about to fall,
      but the LORD helped me.
14 The LORD is my strength and my defense;
      he has become my salvation.

15 Shouts of joy and victory
      resound in the tents of the righteous:
    "The LORD's right hand has done mighty
          things!
16   The LORD's right hand is lifted high;
      the LORD's right hand has done mighty
          things!"
17 I will not die but live,
      and will proclaim what the LORD has
          done.
18 The LORD has chastened me severely,
      but he has not given me over to death.
19 Open for me the gates of the righteous;
      I will enter and give thanks to the LORD.
20 This is the gate of the LORD
      through which the righteous may enter.
21 I will give you thanks, for you answered me;
      you have become my salvation.

22 The stone the builders rejected
      has become the cornerstone;
23 the LORD has done this,
      and it is marvelous in our eyes.

24   The LORD has done it this very day;
        let us rejoice today and be glad.

25   LORD, save us!
        LORD, grant us success!

26   Blessed is he who comes in the name of the
        LORD.
        From the house of the LORD we bless you.
27   The LORD is God,
        and he has made his light shine on us.
    With boughs in hand, join in the festal
        procession
        up to the horns of the altar.

28   You are my God, and I will praise you;
        you are my God, and I will exalt you.

29   Give thanks to the LORD, for he is good;
        his love endures forever.

PSALM 119

א ALEPH

1 Blessed are those whose ways are blameless,
　　who walk according to the law of the
　　　LORD.
2 Blessed are those who keep his statutes
　　and seek him with all their heart —
3 they do no wrong
　　but follow his ways.
4 You have laid down precepts
　　that are to be fully obeyed.
5 Oh, that my ways were steadfast
　　in obeying your decrees!
6 Then I would not be put to shame
　　when I consider all your commands.
7 I will praise you with an upright heart
　　as I learn your righteous laws.
8 I will obey your decrees;
　　do not utterly forsake me.

ב BETH

9 How can a young person stay on the path
　　　of purity?
　　By living according to your word.
10 I seek you with all my heart;
　　do not let me stray from your commands.
11 I have hidden your word in my heart
　　that I might not sin against you.

12 Praise be to you, LORD;
    teach me your decrees.
13 With my lips I recount
    all the laws that come from your mouth.
14 I rejoice in following your statutes
    as one rejoices in great riches.
15 I meditate on your precepts
    and consider your ways.
16 I delight in your decrees;
    I will not neglect your word.

ג GIMEL

17 Be good to your servant while I live,
    that I may obey your word.
18 Open my eyes that I may see
    wonderful things in your law.
19 I am a stranger on earth;
    do not hide your commands from me.
20 My soul is consumed with longing
    for your laws at all times.
21 You rebuke the arrogant, who are accursed,
    those who stray from your commands.
22 Remove from me their scorn and contempt,
    for I keep your statutes.
23 Though rulers sit together and slander me,
    your servant will meditate on your decrees.
24 Your statutes are my delight;
    they are my counselors.

ד DALETH

25 I am laid low in the dust;
    preserve my life according to your word.

26 I gave an account of my ways and you
        answered me;
    teach me your decrees.
27 Cause me to understand the way of your
        precepts,
    that I may meditate on your wonderful
        deeds.
28 My soul is weary with sorrow;
    strengthen me according to your word.
29 Keep me from deceitful ways;
    be gracious to me and teach me your law.
30 I have chosen the way of faithfulness;
    I have set my heart on your laws.
31 I hold fast to your statutes, LORD;
    do not let me be put to shame.
32 I run in the path of your commands,
    for you have broadened my understanding.

ה HE

33 Teach me, LORD, the way of your decrees,
    that I may follow it to the end.
34 Give me understanding, so that I may keep
        your law
    and obey it with all my heart.
35 Direct me in the path of your commands,
    for there I find delight.
36 Turn my heart toward your statutes
    and not toward selfish gain.
37 Turn my eyes away from worthless things;
    preserve my life according to your
        word.

38 Fulfill your promise to your servant,
      so that you may be feared.
39 Take away the disgrace I dread,
      for your laws are good.
40 How I long for your precepts!
      In your righteousness preserve my life.

ו WAW

41 May your unfailing love come to me, LORD,
      your salvation, according to your promise;
42 then I can answer anyone who taunts me,
      for I trust in your word.
43 Never take your word of truth from my mouth,
      for I have put my hope in your laws.
44 I will always obey your law,
      for ever and ever.
45 I will walk about in freedom,
      for I have sought out your precepts.
46 I will speak of your statutes before kings
      and will not be put to shame,
47 for I delight in your commands
      because I love them.
48 I reach out for your commands, which I love,
      that I may meditate on your decrees.

ז ZAYIN

49 Remember your word to your servant,
      for you have given me hope.
50 My comfort in my suffering is this:
      Your promise preserves my life.
51 The arrogant mock me unmercifully,
      but I do not turn from your law.

52 I remember, LORD, your ancient laws,
    and I find comfort in them.
53 Indignation grips me because of the wicked,
    who have forsaken your law.
54 Your decrees are the theme of my song
    wherever I lodge.
55 In the night, LORD, I remember your name,
    that I may keep your law.
56 This has been my practice:
    I obey your precepts.

ח HETH

57 You are my portion, LORD;
    I have promised to obey your words.
58 I have sought your face with all my heart;
    be gracious to me according to your promise.
59 I have considered my ways
    and have turned my steps to your statutes.
60 I will hasten and not delay
    to obey your commands.
61 Though the wicked bind me with ropes,
    I will not forget your law.
62 At midnight I rise to give you thanks
    for your righteous laws.
63 I am a friend to all who fear you,
    to all who follow your precepts.
64 The earth is filled with your love, LORD;
    teach me your decrees.

ט TETH

65 Do good to your servant
    according to your word, LORD.

66 Teach me knowledge and good judgment,
  for I trust your commands.
67 Before I was afflicted I went astray,
  but now I obey your word.
68 You are good, and what you do is good;
  teach me your decrees.
69 Though the arrogant have smeared me with
    lies,
  I keep your precepts with all my heart.
70 Their hearts are callous and unfeeling,
  but I delight in your law.
71 It was good for me to be afflicted
  so that I might learn your decrees.
72 The law from your mouth is more precious
    to me
  than thousands of pieces of silver and gold.

 י YODH

73 Your hands made me and formed me;
  give me understanding to learn your
    commands.
74 May those who fear you rejoice when they
    see me,
  for I have put my hope in your word.
75 I know, LORD, that your laws are righteous,
  and that in faithfulness you have
    afflicted me.
76 May your unfailing love be my comfort,
  according to your promise to your servant.
77 Let your compassion come to me that I may
    live,
  for your law is my delight.

78   May the arrogant be put to shame for wronging
            me without cause;
        but I will meditate on your precepts.
79   May those who fear you turn to me,
        those who understand your statutes.
80   May I wholeheartedly follow your decrees,
        that I may not be put to shame.

כ KAPH

81   My soul faints with longing for your
            salvation,
        but I have put my hope in your word.
82   My eyes fail, looking for your promise;
        I say, "When will you comfort me?"
83   Though I am like a wineskin in the smoke,
        I do not forget your decrees.
84   How long must your servant wait?
        When will you punish my persecutors?
85   The arrogant dig pits to trap me,
        contrary to your law.
86   All your commands are trustworthy;
        help me, for I am being persecuted without
            cause.
87   They almost wiped me from the earth,
        but I have not forsaken your precepts.
88   In your unfailing love preserve my life,
        that I may obey the statutes of your
            mouth.

ל LAMEDH

89   Your word, LORD, is eternal;
        it stands firm in the heavens.

90 Your faithfulness continues through all
generations;
you established the earth, and it endures.
91 Your laws endure to this day,
for all things serve you.
92 If your law had not been my delight,
I would have perished in my affliction.
93 I will never forget your precepts,
for by them you have preserved my life.
94 Save me, for I am yours;
I have sought out your precepts.
95 The wicked are waiting to destroy me,
but I will ponder your statutes.
96 To all perfection I see a limit,
but your commands are boundless.

מ MEM

97 Oh, how I love your law!
I meditate on it all day long.
98 Your commands are always with me
and make me wiser than my enemies.
99 I have more insight than all my teachers,
for I meditate on your statutes.
100 I have more understanding than the elders,
for I obey your precepts.
101 I have kept my feet from every evil path
so that I might obey your word.
102 I have not departed from your laws,
for you yourself have taught me.
103 How sweet are your words to my taste,
sweeter than honey to my mouth!

104 I gain understanding from your precepts;
therefore I hate every wrong path.

ב NUN

105 Your word is a lamp for my feet,
a light on my path.
106 I have taken an oath and confirmed it,
that I will follow your righteous laws.
107 I have suffered much;
preserve my life, LORD, according to your
word.
108 Accept, LORD, the willing praise of my mouth,
and teach me your laws.
109 Though I constantly take my life in my hands,
I will not forget your law.
110 The wicked have set a snare for me,
but I have not strayed from your precepts.
111 Your statutes are my heritage forever;
they are the joy of my heart.
112 My heart is set on keeping your decrees
to the very end.

ס SAMEKH

113 I hate double-minded people,
but I love your law.
114 You are my refuge and my shield;
I have put my hope in your word.
115 Away from me, you evildoers,
that I may keep the commands of my God!
116 Sustain me, my God, according to your
promise, and I will live;
do not let my hopes be dashed.

117 Uphold me, and I will be delivered;
    I will always have regard for your decrees.
118 You reject all who stray from your decrees,
    for their delusions come to nothing.
119 All the wicked of the earth you discard like
        dross;
    therefore I love your statutes.
120 My flesh trembles in fear of you;
    I stand in awe of your laws.

ע AYIN

121 I have done what is righteous and just;
    do not leave me to my oppressors.
122 Ensure your servant's well-being;
    do not let the arrogant oppress me.
123 My eyes fail, looking for your salvation,
    looking for your righteous promise.
124 Deal with your servant according to your
        love
    and teach me your decrees.
125 I am your servant; give me discernment
    that I may understand your statutes.
126 It is time for you to act, LORD;
    your law is being broken.
127 Because I love your commands
    more than gold, more than pure gold,
128 and because I consider all your precepts right,
    I hate every wrong path.

פ PE

129 Your statutes are wonderful;
    therefore I obey them.

130   The unfolding of your words gives light;
      it gives understanding to the simple.
131   I open my mouth and pant,
      longing for your commands.
132   Turn to me and have mercy on me,
      as you always do to those who love your
        name.
133   Direct my footsteps according to your word;
      let no sin rule over me.
134   Redeem me from human oppression,
      that I may obey your precepts.
135   Make your face shine on your servant
      and teach me your decrees.
136   Streams of tears flow from my eyes,
      for your law is not obeyed.

צ TSADHE

137   You are righteous, LORD,
      and your laws are right.
138   The statutes you have laid down are righteous;
      they are fully trustworthy.
139   My zeal wears me out,
      for my enemies ignore your words.
140   Your promises have been thoroughly tested,
      and your servant loves them.
141   Though I am lowly and despised,
      I do not forget your precepts.
142   Your righteousness is everlasting
      and your law is true.
143   Trouble and distress have come upon me,
      but your commands give me delight.

144 Your statutes are always righteous;
    give me understanding that I may live.

ק QOPH

145 I call with all my heart; answer me, Lord,
    and I will obey your decrees.
146 I call out to you; save me
    and I will keep your statutes.
147 I rise before dawn and cry for help;
    I have put my hope in your word.
148 My eyes stay open through the watches of the
    night,
    that I may meditate on your promises.
149 Hear my voice in accordance with your love;
    preserve my life, Lord, according to your
    laws.
150 Those who devise wicked schemes are near,
    but they are far from your law.
151 Yet you are near, Lord,
    and all your commands are true.
152 Long ago I learned from your statutes
    that you established them to last forever.

ר RESH

153 Look on my suffering and deliver me,
    for I have not forgotten your law.
154 Defend my cause and redeem me;
    preserve my life according to your promise.
155 Salvation is far from the wicked,
    for they do not seek out your decrees.
156 Your compassion, Lord, is great;
    preserve my life according to your laws.

157 Many are the foes who persecute me,
　　but I have not turned from your statutes.
158 I look on the faithless with loathing,
　　for they do not obey your word.
159 See how I love your precepts;
　　preserve my life, LORD, in accordance with
　　　your love.
160 All your words are true;
　　all your righteous laws are eternal.

‬שׁ SIN AND SHIN

161 Rulers persecute me without cause,
　　but my heart trembles at your word.
162 I rejoice in your promise
　　like one who finds great spoil.
163 I hate and detest falsehood
　　but I love your law.
164 Seven times a day I praise you
　　for your righteous laws.
165 Great peace have those who love your law,
　　and nothing can make them stumble.
166 I wait for your salvation, LORD,
　　and I follow your commands.
167 I obey your statutes,
　　for I love them greatly.
168 I obey your precepts and your statutes,
　　for all my ways are known to you.

‬ת TAW

169 May my cry come before you, LORD;
　　give me understanding according to your
　　　word.

170 May my supplication come before you;
　　　deliver me according to your promise.
171 May my lips overflow with praise,
　　　for you teach me your decrees.
172 May my tongue sing of your word,
　　　for all your commands are righteous.
173 May your hand be ready to help me,
　　　for I have chosen your precepts.
174 I long for your salvation, Lord,
　　　and your law gives me delight.
175 Let me live that I may praise you,
　　　and may your laws sustain me.
176 I have strayed like a lost sheep.
　　　Seek your servant,
　　　　for I have not forgotten your commands.

PSALM 120

A song of ascents.

1   I call on the LORD in my distress,
      and he answers me.
2   Save me, LORD,
      from lying lips
      and from deceitful tongues.

3   What will he do to you,
      and what more besides,
      you deceitful tongue?
4   He will punish you with a warrior's sharp
        arrows,
      with burning coals of the broom bush.

5   Woe to me that I dwell in Meshek,
      that I live among the tents of Kedar!
6   Too long have I lived
      among those who hate peace.
7   I am for peace;
      but when I speak, they are for war.

PSALM 121

A song of ascents.

1   I lift up my eyes to the mountains —
       where does my help come from?
2   My help comes from the LORD,
       the Maker of heaven and earth.

3   He will not let your foot slip —
       he who watches over you will not slumber;
4   indeed, he who watches over Israel
       will neither slumber nor sleep.

5   The LORD watches over you —
       the LORD is your shade at your right hand;
6   the sun will not harm you by day,
       nor the moon by night.

7   The LORD will keep you from all harm —
       he will watch over your life;
8   the LORD will watch over your coming and
               going
       both now and forevermore.

PSALM 122

A song of ascents. Of David.

1   I rejoiced with those who said to me,
        "Let us go to the house of the LORD."
2   Our feet are standing
        in your gates, Jerusalem.

3   Jerusalem is built like a city
        that is closely compacted together.
4   That is where the tribes go up —
        the tribes of the LORD —
    to praise the name of the LORD
        according to the statute given to Israel.
5   There stand the thrones for judgment,
        the thrones of the house of David.

6   Pray for the peace of Jerusalem:
        "May those who love you be secure.
7   May there be peace within your walls
        and security within your citadels."
8   For the sake of my family and friends,
        I will say, "Peace be within you."
9   For the sake of the house of the LORD our God,
        I will seek your prosperity.

PSALM 123

A song of ascents.

1   I lift up my eyes to you,
        to you who sit enthroned in heaven.
2   As the eyes of slaves look to the hand of their
                master,
            as the eyes of a female slave look to the hand
                of her mistress,
        so our eyes look to the LORD our God,
            till he shows us his mercy.

3   Have mercy on us, LORD, have mercy on us,
        for we have endured no end of contempt.
4   We have endured no end
        of ridicule from the arrogant,
        of contempt from the proud.

PSALM 124

A song of ascents. Of David.

1 If the LORD had not been on our side —
    let Israel say —
2 if the LORD had not been on our side
    when people attacked us,
3 they would have swallowed us alive
    when their anger flared against us;
4 the flood would have engulfed us,
    the torrent would have swept over us,
5 the raging waters
    would have swept us away.

6 Praise be to the LORD,
    who has not let us be torn by their teeth.
7 We have escaped like a bird
    from the fowler's snare;
the snare has been broken,
    and we have escaped.
8 Our help is in the name of the LORD,
    the Maker of heaven and earth.

PSALM 125

A song of ascents.

1   Those who trust in the LORD are like Mount
        Zion,
        which cannot be shaken but endures forever.
2   As the mountains surround Jerusalem,
        so the LORD surrounds his people
        both now and forevermore.

3   The scepter of the wicked will not remain
        over the land allotted to the righteous,
    for then the righteous might use
        their hands to do evil.

4   LORD, do good to those who are good,
        to those who are upright in heart.
5   But those who turn to crooked ways
        the LORD will banish with the evildoers.

    Peace be on Israel.

PSALM 126

A song of ascents.

1   When the LORD restored the fortunes of Zion,
        we were like those who dreamed.
2   Our mouths were filled with laughter,
        our tongues with songs of joy.
    Then it was said among the nations,
        "The LORD has done great things for them."
3   The LORD has done great things for us,
        and we are filled with joy.

4   Restore our fortunes, LORD,
        like streams in the Negev.
5   Those who sow with tears
        will reap with songs of joy.
6   Those who go out weeping,
        carrying seed to sow,
    will return with songs of joy,
        carrying sheaves with them.

PSALM 127

A song of ascents. Of Solomon.

1   Unless the LORD builds the house,
        the builders labor in vain.
    Unless the LORD watches over the city,
        the guards stand watch in vain.
2   In vain you rise early
        and stay up late,
    toiling for food to eat —
        for he grants sleep to those he loves.

3   Children are a heritage from the LORD,
        offspring a reward from him.
4   Like arrows in the hands of a warrior
        are children born in one's youth.
5   Blessed is the man
        whose quiver is full of them.
    They will not be put to shame
        when they contend with their opponents in
            court.

PSALM 128

A song of ascents.

1 Blessed are all who fear the LORD,
   who walk in obedience to him.
2 You will eat the fruit of your labor;
   blessings and prosperity will be yours.
3 Your wife will be like a fruitful vine
   within your house;
   your children will be like olive shoots
   around your table.
4 Yes, this will be the blessing
   for the man who fears the LORD.

5 May the LORD bless you from Zion;
   may you see the prosperity of Jerusalem
   all the days of your life.
6 May you live to see your children's children —
   peace be on Israel.

PSALM 129

A song of ascents.

1 "They have greatly oppressed me from my
 youth,"
  let Israel say;
2 "they have greatly oppressed me from my
 youth,
  but they have not gained the victory
  over me.
3 Plowmen have plowed my back
  and made their furrows long.
4 But the LORD is righteous;
  he has cut me free from the cords of the
  wicked."

5 May all who hate Zion
  be turned back in shame.
6 May they be like grass on the roof,
  which withers before it can grow;
7 a reaper cannot fill his hands with it,
  nor one who gathers fill his arms.
8 May those who pass by not say to them,
  "The blessing of the LORD be on you;
  we bless you in the name of the LORD."

PSALM 130

A song of ascents.

1 Out of the depths I cry to you, Lord;
2   Lord, hear my voice.
   Let your ears be attentive
       to my cry for mercy.

3 If you, Lord, kept a record of sins,
       Lord, who could stand?
4 But with you there is forgiveness,
       so that we can, with reverence, serve you.

5 I wait for the Lord, my whole being waits,
       and in his word I put my hope.
6 I wait for the Lord
       more than watchmen wait for the morning,
       more than watchmen wait for the morning.

7 Israel, put your hope in the Lord,
       for with the Lord is unfailing love
       and with him is full redemption.
8 He himself will redeem Israel
       from all their sins.

PSALM 131

A song of ascents. Of David.

1 My heart is not proud, Lord,
   my eyes are not haughty;
I do not concern myself with great matters
   or things too wonderful for me.
2 But I have calmed and quieted myself,
   I am like a weaned child with its mother;
   like a weaned child I am content.

3 Israel, put your hope in the Lord
   both now and forevermore.

PSALM 132

A song of ascents.

1   Lord, remember David
      and all his self-denial.

2   He swore an oath to the Lord,
      he made a vow to the Mighty One of
          Jacob:
3   "I will not enter my house
      or go to my bed,
4   I will allow no sleep to my eyes
      or slumber to my eyelids,
5   till I find a place for the Lord,
      a dwelling for the Mighty One of Jacob."

6   We heard it in Ephrathah,
      we came upon it in the fields of Jaar:
7   "Let us go to his dwelling place,
      let us worship at his footstool, saying,
8   'Arise, Lord, and come to your resting place,
      you and the ark of your might.
9   May your priests be clothed with your
          righteousness;
      may your faithful people sing for joy.'"

10   For the sake of your servant David,
      do not reject your anointed one.

11   The Lord swore an oath to David,
      a sure oath he will not revoke:

"One of your own descendants
I will place on your throne.
12 If your sons keep my covenant
and the statutes I teach them,
then their sons will sit
on your throne for ever and ever."

13 For the LORD has chosen Zion,
he has desired it for his dwelling, saying,
14 "This is my resting place for ever and ever;
here I will sit enthroned, for I have
desired it.
15 I will bless her with abundant provisions;
her poor I will satisfy with food.
16 I will clothe her priests with salvation,
and her faithful people will ever sing for joy.

17 "Here I will make a horn grow for David
and set up a lamp for my anointed one.
18 I will clothe his enemies with shame,
but his head will be adorned with a radiant
crown."

PSALM 133

A song of ascents. Of David.

1   How good and pleasant it is
         when God's people live together in unity!

2   It is like precious oil poured on the head,
         running down on the beard,
     running down on Aaron's beard,
         down on the collar of his robe.
3   It is as if the dew of Hermon
         were falling on Mount Zion.
     For there the Lord bestows his blessing,
         even life forevermore.

PSALM 134

A song of ascents.

1 Praise the LORD, all you servants of the
   LORD
      who minister by night in the house of the
      LORD.
2 Lift up your hands in the sanctuary
      and praise the LORD.

3 May the LORD bless you from Zion,
      he who is the Maker of heaven and earth.

PSALM 135

1   Praise the LORD.

Praise the name of the LORD;
    praise him, you servants of the LORD,
2   you who minister in the house of the LORD,
    in the courts of the house of our God.

3   Praise the LORD, for the LORD is good;
    sing praise to his name, for that is
        pleasant.
4   For the LORD has chosen Jacob to be his own,
    Israel to be his treasured possession.

5   I know that the LORD is great,
    that our Lord is greater than all gods.
6   The LORD does whatever pleases him,
    in the heavens and on the earth,
    in the seas and all their depths.
7   He makes clouds rise from the ends of the
        earth;
    he sends lightning with the rain
    and brings out the wind from his
        storehouses.

8   He struck down the firstborn of Egypt,
    the firstborn of people and animals.
9   He sent his signs and wonders into your midst,
        Egypt,
    against Pharaoh and all his servants.

10   He struck down many nations
           and killed mighty kings —
11   Sihon king of the Amorites,
           Og king of Bashan,
           and all the kings of Canaan —
12   and he gave their land as an inheritance,
           an inheritance to his people Israel.

13   Your name, Lord, endures forever,
           your renown, Lord, through all generations.
14   For the Lord will vindicate his people
           and have compassion on his servants.

15   The idols of the nations are silver and gold,
           made by human hands.
16   They have mouths, but cannot speak,
           eyes, but cannot see.
17   They have ears, but cannot hear,
           nor is there breath in their mouths.
18   Those who make them will be like them,
           and so will all who trust in them.

19   All you Israelites, praise the Lord;
           house of Aaron, praise the Lord;
20   house of Levi, praise the Lord;
           you who fear him, praise the Lord.
21   Praise be to the Lord from Zion,
           to him who dwells in Jerusalem.

       Praise the Lord.

PSALM 136

1   Give thanks to the Lᴏʀᴅ, for he is good.
> *His love endures forever.*

2   Give thanks to the God of gods.
> *His love endures forever.*

3   Give thanks to the Lord of lords:
> *His love endures forever.*

4   to him who alone does great wonders,
> *His love endures forever.*

5   who by his understanding made the heavens,
> *His love endures forever.*

6   who spread out the earth upon the waters,
> *His love endures forever.*

7   who made the great lights —
> *His love endures forever.*

8   the sun to govern the day,
> *His love endures forever.*

9   the moon and stars to govern the night;
> *His love endures forever.*

10 to him who struck down the firstborn of Egypt
> *His love endures forever.*

11 and brought Israel out from among them
> *His love endures forever.*

12 with a mighty hand and outstretched arm;
> *His love endures forever.*

13 to him who divided the Red Sea asunder
> *His love endures forever.*

14   and brought Israel through the midst of it,
His love endures forever.

15   but swept Pharaoh and his army into the Red
      Sea;
His love endures forever.

16   to him who led his people through the
      wilderness;
His love endures forever.

17   to him who struck down great kings,
His love endures forever.

18   and killed mighty kings —
His love endures forever.

19   Sihon king of the Amorites
His love endures forever.

20   and Og king of Bashan —
His love endures forever.

21   and gave their land as an inheritance,
His love endures forever.

22   an inheritance to his servant Israel.
His love endures forever.

23   He remembered us in our low estate
His love endures forever.

24   and freed us from our enemies.
His love endures forever.

25   He gives food to every creature.
His love endures forever.

26   Give thanks to the God of heaven.
His love endures forever.

PSALM 137

1   By the rivers of Babylon we sat and wept
        when we remembered Zion.
2   There on the poplars
        we hung our harps,
3   for there our captors asked us for songs,
        our tormentors demanded songs of joy;
        they said, "Sing us one of the songs of
            Zion!"

4   How can we sing the songs of the LORD
        while in a foreign land?
5   If I forget you, Jerusalem,
        may my right hand forget its skill.
6   May my tongue cling to the roof of my
            mouth
        if I do not remember you,
    if I do not consider Jerusalem
        my highest joy.

7   Remember, LORD, what the Edomites did
        on the day Jerusalem fell.
    "Tear it down," they cried,
        "tear it down to its foundations!"
8   Daughter Babylon, doomed to destruction,
        happy is the one who repays you
        according to what you have done to us.
9   Happy is the one who seizes your infants
        and dashes them against the rocks.

PSALM 138

Of David.

1   I will praise you, LORD, with all my heart;
      before the "gods" I will sing your praise.
2   I will bow down toward your holy temple
      and will praise your name
      for your unfailing love and your faithfulness,
   for you have so exalted your solemn decree
      that it surpasses your fame.
3   When I called, you answered me;
      you greatly emboldened me.

4   May all the kings of the earth praise you, LORD,
      when they hear what you have decreed.
5   May they sing of the ways of the LORD,
      for the glory of the LORD is great.

6   Though the LORD is exalted, he looks kindly on
      the lowly;
      though lofty, he sees them from afar.
7   Though I walk in the midst of trouble,
      you preserve my life.
   You stretch out your hand against the anger of
      my foes;
      with your right hand you save me.
8   The LORD will vindicate me;
      your love, LORD, endures forever —
      do not abandon the works of your hands.

PSALM 139

For the director of music.
Of David. A psalm.

1   You have searched me, LORD,
        and you know me.
2   You know when I sit and when I rise;
        you perceive my thoughts from afar.
3   You discern my going out and my lying
            down;
        you are familiar with all my ways.
4   Before a word is on my tongue
        you, LORD, know it completely.
5   You hem me in behind and before,
        and you lay your hand upon me.
6   Such knowledge is too wonderful for me,
        too lofty for me to attain.

7   Where can I go from your Spirit?
        Where can I flee from your presence?
8   If I go up to the heavens, you are there;
        if I make my bed in the depths, you are
            there.
9   If I rise on the wings of the dawn,
        if I settle on the far side of the sea,
10 even there your hand will guide me,
        your right hand will hold me fast.
11 If I say, "Surely the darkness will hide me
        and the light become night around me,"

12   even the darkness will not be dark to you;
      the night will shine like the day,
      for darkness is as light to you.

13   For you created my inmost being;
      you knit me together in my mother's womb.

14   I praise you because I am fearfully and
       wonderfully made;
      your works are wonderful,
      I know that full well.

15   My frame was not hidden from you
      when I was made in the secret place,
      when I was woven together in the depths
       of the earth.

16   Your eyes saw my unformed body;
      all the days ordained for me were written
       in your book
      before one of them came to be.

17   How precious to me are your thoughts, God!
      How vast is the sum of them!

18   Were I to count them,
      they would outnumber the grains of
       sand—
      when I awake, I am still with you.

19   If only you, God, would slay the wicked!
      Away from me, you who are bloodthirsty!

20   They speak of you with evil intent;
      your adversaries misuse your name.

21   Do I not hate those who hate you, LORD,
      and abhor those who are in rebellion
       against you?

22   I have nothing but hatred for them;
        I count them my enemies.
23   Search me, God, and know my heart;
        test me and know my anxious thoughts.
24   See if there is any offensive way in me,
        and lead me in the way everlasting.

PSALM 140

For the director of music.
A psalm of David.

1 Rescue me, LORD, from evildoers;
   protect me from the violent,
2 who devise evil plans in their hearts
   and stir up war every day.
3 They make their tongues as sharp as a
      serpent's;
   the poison of vipers is on their lips.

4 Keep me safe, LORD, from the hands of the
      wicked;
   protect me from the violent,
   who devise ways to trip my feet.
5 The arrogant have hidden a snare for me;
   they have spread out the cords of their net
   and have set traps for me along my path.

6 I say to the LORD, "You are my God."
   Hear, LORD, my cry for mercy.
7 Sovereign LORD, my strong deliverer,
   you shield my head in the day of battle.
8 Do not grant the wicked their desires, LORD;
   do not let their plans succeed.

9 Those who surround me proudly rear their
      heads;
   may the mischief of their lips engulf them.

10 May burning coals fall on them;
         may they be thrown into the fire,
         into miry pits, never to rise.
11 May slanderers not be established in the land;
         may disaster hunt down the violent.

12 I know that the LORD secures justice for the
              poor
         and upholds the cause of the needy.
13 Surely the righteous will praise your name,
         and the upright will live in your presence.

PSALM 141

A psalm of David.

1 I call to you, LORD, come quickly to me;
    hear me when I call to you.
2 May my prayer be set before you like incense;
    may the lifting up of my hands be like the
        evening sacrifice.

3 Set a guard over my mouth, LORD;
    keep watch over the door of my lips.
4 Do not let my heart be drawn to what is evil
    so that I take part in wicked deeds
along with those who are evildoers;
    do not let me eat their delicacies.

5 Let a righteous man strike me — that is a
        kindness;
    let him rebuke me — that is oil on my head.
My head will not refuse it,
    for my prayer will still be against the deeds
        of evildoers.

6 Their rulers will be thrown down from the cliffs,
    and the wicked will learn that my words
        were well spoken.
7 They will say, "As one plows and breaks up the
        earth,
    so our bones have been scattered at the
        mouth of the grave."

8   But my eyes are fixed on you, Sovereign LORD;
        in you I take refuge — do not give me over to
            death.
9   Keep me safe from the traps set by evildoers,
        from the snares they have laid for me.
10 Let the wicked fall into their own nets,
        while I pass by in safety.

PSALM 142

*A maskil of David. When he was
in the cave. A prayer.*

1 I cry aloud to the LORD;
     I lift up my voice to the LORD for mercy.
2 I pour out before him my complaint;
     before him I tell my trouble.

3 When my spirit grows faint within me,
     it is you who watch over my way.
   In the path where I walk
     people have hidden a snare for me.
4 Look and see, there is no one at my right hand;
     no one is concerned for me.
   I have no refuge;
     no one cares for my life.

5 I cry to you, LORD;
     I say, "You are my refuge,
     my portion in the land of the living."

6 Listen to my cry,
     for I am in desperate need;
   rescue me from those who pursue me,
     for they are too strong for me.
7 Set me free from my prison,
     that I may praise your name.
   Then the righteous will gather about me
     because of your goodness to me.

PSALM 143

A psalm of David.

1 LORD, hear my prayer,
    listen to my cry for mercy;
in your faithfulness and righteousness
    come to my relief.
2 Do not bring your servant into judgment,
    for no one living is righteous before you.
3 The enemy pursues me,
    he crushes me to the ground;
he makes me dwell in the darkness
    like those long dead.
4 So my spirit grows faint within me;
    my heart within me is dismayed.
5 I remember the days of long ago;
    I meditate on all your works
    and consider what your hands have done.
6 I spread out my hands to you;
    I thirst for you like a parched land.

7 Answer me quickly, LORD;
    my spirit fails.
Do not hide your face from me
    or I will be like those who go down to
        the pit.
8 Let the morning bring me word of your
        unfailing love,
    for I have put my trust in you.

Show me the way I should go,
    for to you I entrust my life.
9 Rescue me from my enemies, LORD,
    for I hide myself in you.
10 Teach me to do your will,
    for you are my God;
may your good Spirit
    lead me on level ground.

11 For your name's sake, LORD, preserve my life;
    in your righteousness, bring me out of
        trouble.
12 In your unfailing love, silence my enemies;
    destroy all my foes,
    for I am your servant.

PSALM 144

Of David.

1 Praise be to the Lord my Rock,
    who trains my hands for war,
    my fingers for battle.
2 He is my loving God and my fortress,
    my stronghold and my deliverer,
  my shield, in whom I take refuge,
    who subdues peoples under me.

3 Lord, what are human beings that you care for
      them,
    mere mortals that you think of them?
4 They are like a breath;
    their days are like a fleeting shadow.

5 Part your heavens, Lord, and come down;
    touch the mountains, so that they smoke.
6 Send forth lightning and scatter the enemy;
    shoot your arrows and rout them.
7 Reach down your hand from on high;
    deliver me and rescue me
  from the mighty waters,
    from the hands of foreigners
8 whose mouths are full of lies,
    whose right hands are deceitful.

9 I will sing a new song to you, my God;
    on the ten-stringed lyre I will make music to
      you,

10   to the One who gives victory to kings,
            who delivers his servant David.

        From the deadly sword
11   deliver me;
            rescue me from the hands of foreigners
        whose mouths are full of lies,
            whose right hands are deceitful.

12   Then our sons in their youth
            will be like well-nurtured plants,
        and our daughters will be like pillars
            carved to adorn a palace.
13   Our barns will be filled
            with every kind of provision.
        Our sheep will increase by thousands,
            by tens of thousands in our fields;
14   our oxen will draw heavy loads.
        There will be no breaching of walls,
            no going into captivity,
            no cry of distress in our streets.
15   Blessed is the people of whom this is true;
            blessed is the people whose God is the Lord.

PSALM 145

A psalm of praise. Of David.

1   I will exalt you, my God the King;
      I will praise your name for ever and ever.
2   Every day I will praise you
      and extol your name for ever and ever.

3   Great is the LORD and most worthy of praise;
      his greatness no one can fathom.
4   One generation commends your works to
            another;
      they tell of your mighty acts.
5   They speak of the glorious splendor of your
            majesty —
      and I will meditate on your wonderful
            works.
6   They tell of the power of your awesome
            works —
      and I will proclaim your great deeds.
7   They celebrate your abundant goodness
      and joyfully sing of your righteousness.

8   The LORD is gracious and compassionate,
      slow to anger and rich in love.

9   The LORD is good to all;
      he has compassion on all he has made.
10 All your works praise you, LORD;
      your faithful people extol you.

11 They tell of the glory of your kingdom
and speak of your might,
12 so that all people may know of your mighty
acts
and the glorious splendor of your kingdom.
13 Your kingdom is an everlasting kingdom,
and your dominion endures through all
generations.

The Lord is trustworthy in all he promises
and faithful in all he does.
14 The Lord upholds all who fall
and lifts up all who are bowed down.
15 The eyes of all look to you,
and you give them their food at the proper
time.
16 You open your hand
and satisfy the desires of every living
thing.

17 The Lord is righteous in all his ways
and faithful in all he does.
18 The Lord is near to all who call on him,
to all who call on him in truth.
19 He fulfills the desires of those who fear him;
he hears their cry and saves them.
20 The Lord watches over all who love him,
but all the wicked he will destroy.

21 My mouth will speak in praise of the Lord.
Let every creature praise his holy name
for ever and ever.

PSALM 146

1   Praise the LORD.

     Praise the LORD, my soul.

2   I will praise the LORD all my life;
        I will sing praise to my God as long as I live.

3   Do not put your trust in princes,
        in human beings, who cannot save.

4   When their spirit departs, they return to the
            ground;
        on that very day their plans come to
            nothing.

5   Blessed are those whose help is the God of
            Jacob,
        whose hope is in the LORD their God.

6   He is the Maker of heaven and earth,
        the sea, and everything in them —
        he remains faithful forever.

7   He upholds the cause of the oppressed
        and gives food to the hungry.
     The LORD sets prisoners free,

8   the LORD gives sight to the blind,
   the LORD lifts up those who are bowed down,
        the LORD loves the righteous.

9   The LORD watches over the foreigner
        and sustains the fatherless and the widow,
        but he frustrates the ways of the wicked.

10   The LORD reigns forever,
        your God, O Zion, for all generations.

Praise the LORD.

PSALM 147

1 Praise the LORD.

How good it is to sing praises to our God,
how pleasant and fitting to praise him!

2 The LORD builds up Jerusalem;
he gathers the exiles of Israel.
3 He heals the brokenhearted
and binds up their wounds.
4 He determines the number of the stars
and calls them each by name.
5 Great is our Lord and mighty in power;
his understanding has no limit.
6 The LORD sustains the humble
but casts the wicked to the ground.

7 Sing to the LORD with grateful praise;
make music to our God on the harp.

8 He covers the sky with clouds;
he supplies the earth with rain
and makes grass grow on the hills.
9 He provides food for the cattle
and for the young ravens when they call.

10 His pleasure is not in the strength of the horse,
nor his delight in the legs of the warrior;
11 the LORD delights in those who fear him,
who put their hope in his unfailing love.

12   Extol the LORD, Jerusalem;
          praise your God, Zion.

13   He strengthens the bars of your gates
          and blesses your people within you.
14   He grants peace to your borders
          and satisfies you with the finest of wheat.

15   He sends his command to the earth;
          his word runs swiftly.
16   He spreads the snow like wool
          and scatters the frost like ashes.
17   He hurls down his hail like pebbles.
          Who can withstand his icy blast?
18   He sends his word and melts them;
          he stirs up his breezes, and the waters flow.

19   He has revealed his word to Jacob,
          his laws and decrees to Israel.
20   He has done this for no other nation;
          they do not know his laws.

      Praise the LORD.

....

....

....

....

....

....

PSALM 148

1 Praise the LORD.

Praise the LORD from the heavens;
  praise him in the heights above.
2 Praise him, all his angels;
  praise him, all his heavenly hosts.
3 Praise him, sun and moon;
  praise him, all you shining stars.
4 Praise him, you highest heavens
  and you waters above the skies.

5 Let them praise the name of the LORD,
  for at his command they were created,
6 and he established them for ever and ever —
  he issued a decree that will never pass away.

7 Praise the LORD from the earth,
  you great sea creatures and all ocean
    depths,
8 lightning and hail, snow and clouds,
  stormy winds that do his bidding,
9 you mountains and all hills,
  fruit trees and all cedars,
10 wild animals and all cattle,
  small creatures and flying birds,
11 kings of the earth and all nations,
  you princes and all rulers on earth,
12 young men and women,
  old men and children.

13   Let them praise the name of the LORD,
       for his name alone is exalted;
       his splendor is above the earth and the
         heavens.
14   And he has raised up for his people a horn,
       the praise of all his faithful servants,
       of Israel, the people close to his heart.

Praise the LORD.

PSALM 149

1   Praise the LORD.

    Sing to the LORD a new song,
        his praise in the assembly of his faithful
            people.

2   Let Israel rejoice in their Maker;
        let the people of Zion be glad in their
            King.

3   Let them praise his name with dancing
        and make music to him with timbrel
            and harp.

4   For the LORD takes delight in his people;
        he crowns the humble with victory.

5   Let his faithful people rejoice in this honor
        and sing for joy on their beds.

6   May the praise of God be in their mouths
        and a double-edged sword in their hands,

7   to inflict vengeance on the nations
        and punishment on the peoples,

8   to bind their kings with fetters,
        their nobles with shackles of iron,

9   to carry out the sentence written against
            them —
        this is the glory of all his faithful people.

    Praise the LORD.

PSALM 150

1   Praise the LORD.

Praise God in his sanctuary;
    praise him in his mighty heavens.
2   Praise him for his acts of power;
    praise him for his surpassing greatness.
3   Praise him with the sounding of the trumpet,
    praise him with the harp and lyre,
4   praise him with timbrel and dancing,
    praise him with the strings and pipe,
5   praise him with the clash of cymbals,
    praise him with resounding cymbals.

6   Let everything that has breath praise the LORD.

Praise the LORD.

PROVERBS

WHAT IS A PROVERB?

The book of Proverbs is just one of sixty-six books of the Holy Bible. The Proverbs are part of the Old Testament of the Bible. Proverbs are a part of the biblical wisdom tradition that asks questions about values and morals and the meaning of life. Some of this wisdom is in the form of short sayings and other parts are longer instructions or pieces of advice. Various authors likely wrote these wise sayings, but the most well-known is King Solomon, who famously asked God for wisdom.

This is a book of commonsense advice for all people. Proverbs give us important understanding and excellent wisdom for how to live a happy and holy life. And we do this first and foremost by honoring God, who is all good and all powerful.

PROVERBS 1

1   The proverbs of Solomon son of David, king of Is-
    rael:

2   for gaining wisdom and instruction;
            for understanding words of insight;
3   for receiving instruction in prudent behavior,
            doing what is right and just and fair;
4   for giving prudence to those who are simple,
            knowledge and discretion to the young —
5   let the wise listen and add to their learning,
            and let the discerning get guidance —
6   for understanding proverbs and parables,
            the sayings and riddles of the wise.

7   The fear of the LORD is the beginning of
                knowledge,
            but fools despise wisdom and instruction.

PROLOGUE: EXHORTATIONS
TO EMBRACE WISDOM

Warning Against the Invitation of Sinful Men

8   Listen, my son, to your father's instruction
            and do not forsake your mother's teaching.
9   They are a garland to grace your head
            and a chain to adorn your neck.

10   My son, if sinful men entice you,
            do not give in to them.

11   If they say, "Come along with us;
       let's lie in wait for innocent blood,
       let's ambush some harmless soul;
12   let's swallow them alive, like the grave,
       and whole, like those who go down to the
          pit;
13   we will get all sorts of valuable things
       and fill our houses with plunder;
14   cast lots with us;
       we will all share the loot" —
15   my son, do not go along with them,
       do not set foot on their paths;
16   for their feet rush into evil,
       they are swift to shed blood.
17   How useless to spread a net
       where every bird can see it!
18   These men lie in wait for their own blood;
       they ambush only themselves!
19   Such are the paths of all who go after ill-gotten
          gain;
       it takes away the life of those who get it.

Wisdom's Rebuke

20   Out in the open wisdom calls aloud,
       she raises her voice in the public square;
21   on top of the wall she cries out,
       at the city gate she makes her speech:

22   "How long will you who are simple love your
          simple ways?
       How long will mockers delight in mockery
       and fools hate knowledge?

23 Repent at my rebuke!
   Then I will pour out my thoughts to you,
   I will make known to you my teachings.
24 But since you refuse to listen when I call
   and no one pays attention when I stretch out
   my hand,
25 since you disregard all my advice
   and do not accept my rebuke,
26 I in turn will laugh when disaster strikes you;
   I will mock when calamity overtakes you —
27 when calamity overtakes you like a storm,
   when disaster sweeps over you like a
   whirlwind,
   when distress and trouble overwhelm you.

28 "Then they will call to me but I will not answer;
   they will look for me but will not find me,
29 since they hated knowledge
   and did not choose to fear the LORD.
30 Since they would not accept my advice
   and spurned my rebuke,
31 they will eat the fruit of their ways
   and be filled with the fruit of their schemes.
32 For the waywardness of the simple will kill
   them,
   and the complacency of fools will destroy
   them;
33 but whoever listens to me will live in safety
   and be at ease, without fear of harm."

PROVERBS 2

Moral Benefits of Wisdom

1   My son, if you accept my words
        and store up my commands within you,
2   turning your ear to wisdom
        and applying your heart to understanding —
3   indeed, if you call out for insight
        and cry aloud for understanding,
4   and if you look for it as for silver
        and search for it as for hidden treasure,
5   then you will understand the fear of the LORD
        and find the knowledge of God.
6   For the LORD gives wisdom;
        from his mouth come knowledge and
            understanding.
7   He holds success in store for the upright,
        he is a shield to those whose walk is
            blameless,
8   for he guards the course of the just
        and protects the way of his faithful ones.

9   Then you will understand what is right and
            just
        and fair — every good path.
10 For wisdom will enter your heart,
        and knowledge will be pleasant to your soul.
11 Discretion will protect you,
        and understanding will guard you.

12   Wisdom will save you from the ways of wicked
              men,
       from men whose words are perverse,
13   who have left the straight paths
       to walk in dark ways,
14   who delight in doing wrong
       and rejoice in the perverseness of evil,
15   whose paths are crooked
       and who are devious in their ways.

16   Wisdom will save you also from the adulterous
              woman,
       from the wayward woman with her
           seductive words,
17   who has left the partner of her youth
       and ignored the covenant she made before
           God.
18   Surely her house leads down to death
       and her paths to the spirits of the dead.
19   None who go to her return
       or attain the paths of life.

20   Thus you will walk in the ways of the good
       and keep to the paths of the righteous.
21   For the upright will live in the land,
       and the blameless will remain in it;
22   but the wicked will be cut off from the land,
       and the unfaithful will be torn from it.

PROVERBS 3

Wisdom Bestows Well-Being

1   My son, do not forget my teaching,
     but keep my commands in your heart,
2   for they will prolong your life many years
     and bring you peace and prosperity.

3   Let love and faithfulness never leave you;
     bind them around your neck,
     write them on the tablet of your heart.
4   Then you will win favor and a good name
     in the sight of God and man.

5   Trust in the Lord with all your heart
     and lean not on your own understanding;
6   in all your ways submit to him,
     and he will make your paths straight.

7   Do not be wise in your own eyes;
     fear the Lord and shun evil.
8   This will bring health to your body
     and nourishment to your bones.

9   Honor the Lord with your wealth,
     with the firstfruits of all your crops;
10   then your barns will be filled to overflowing,
     and your vats will brim over with new wine.

11   My son, do not despise the Lord's discipline,
     and do not resent his rebuke,

12 because the LORD disciplines those he loves,
as a father the son he delights in.

13 Blessed are those who find wisdom,
those who gain understanding,
14 for she is more profitable than silver
and yields better returns than gold.
15 She is more precious than rubies;
nothing you desire can compare with
her.
16 Long life is in her right hand;
in her left hand are riches and honor.
17 Her ways are pleasant ways,
and all her paths are peace.
18 She is a tree of life to those who take hold
of her;
those who hold her fast will be blessed.

19 By wisdom the LORD laid the earth's
foundations,
by understanding he set the heavens in
place;
20 by his knowledge the watery depths were
divided,
and the clouds let drop the dew.

21 My son, do not let wisdom and understanding
out of your sight,
preserve sound judgment and discretion;
22 they will be life for you,
an ornament to grace your neck.
23 Then you will go on your way in safety,
and your foot will not stumble.

24 When you lie down, you will not be afraid;
    when you lie down, your sleep will be
    sweet.
25 Have no fear of sudden disaster
    or of the ruin that overtakes the wicked,
26 for the LORD will be at your side
    and will keep your foot from being snared.

27 Do not withhold good from those to whom it
    is due,
    when it is in your power to act.
28 Do not say to your neighbor,
    "Come back tomorrow and I'll give it to
    you" —
    when you already have it with you.
29 Do not plot harm against your neighbor,
    who lives trustfully near you.
30 Do not accuse anyone for no reason —
    when they have done you no harm.

31 Do not envy the violent
    or choose any of their ways.

32 For the LORD detests the perverse
    but takes the upright into his confidence.
33 The LORD's curse is on the house of the wicked,
    but he blesses the home of the righteous.
34 He mocks proud mockers
    but shows favor to the humble and
    oppressed.
35 The wise inherit honor,
    but fools get only shame.

PROVERBS 4

Get Wisdom at Any Cost

1   Listen, my sons, to a father's instruction;
        pay attention and gain understanding.
2   I give you sound learning,
        so do not forsake my teaching.
3   For I too was a son to my father,
        still tender, and cherished by my mother.
4   Then he taught me, and he said to me,
        "Take hold of my words with all your heart;
        keep my commands, and you will live.
5   Get wisdom, get understanding;
        do not forget my words or turn away from
            them.
6   Do not forsake wisdom, and she will protect
            you;
        love her, and she will watch over you.
7   The beginning of wisdom is this: Get wisdom.
        Though it cost all you have, get
            understanding.
8   Cherish her, and she will exalt you;
        embrace her, and she will honor you.
9   She will give you a garland to grace your
            head
        and present you with a glorious crown."

10 Listen, my son, accept what I say,
        and the years of your life will be many.

11   I instruct you in the way of wisdom
        and lead you along straight paths.
12   When you walk, your steps will not be
        hampered;
        when you run, you will not stumble.
13   Hold on to instruction, do not let it go;
        guard it well, for it is your life.
14   Do not set foot on the path of the wicked
        or walk in the way of evildoers.
15   Avoid it, do not travel on it;
        turn from it and go on your way.
16   For they cannot rest until they do evil;
        they are robbed of sleep till they make
        someone stumble.
17   They eat the bread of wickedness
        and drink the wine of violence.

18   The path of the righteous is like the morning
        sun,
        shining ever brighter till the full light
        of day.
19   But the way of the wicked is like deep
        darkness;
        they do not know what makes them
        stumble.

20   My son, pay attention to what I say;
        turn your ear to my words.
21   Do not let them out of your sight,
        keep them within your heart;
22   for they are life to those who find them
        and health to one's whole body.

23   Above all else, guard your heart,
        for everything you do flows from it.
24   Keep your mouth free of perversity;
        keep corrupt talk far from your lips.
25   Let your eyes look straight ahead;
        fix your gaze directly before you.
26   Give careful thought to the paths for your feet
        and be steadfast in all your ways.
27   Do not turn to the right or the left;
        keep your foot from evil.

PROVERBS 5

Warning Against Adultery

1   My son, pay attention to my wisdom,
      turn your ear to my words of insight,

2   that you may maintain discretion
      and your lips may preserve knowledge.

3   For the lips of the adulterous woman drip
      honey,
      and her speech is smoother than oil;

4   but in the end she is bitter as gall,
      sharp as a double-edged sword.

5   Her feet go down to death;
      her steps lead straight to the grave.

6   She gives no thought to the way of life;
      her paths wander aimlessly, but she does
      not know it.

7   Now then, my sons, listen to me;
      do not turn aside from what I say.

8   Keep to a path far from her,
      do not go near the door of her house,

9   lest you lose your honor to others
      and your dignity to one who is cruel,

10   lest strangers feast on your wealth
      and your toil enrich the house of another.

11   At the end of your life you will groan,
      when your flesh and body are spent.

12   You will say, "How I hated discipline!
      How my heart spurned correction!

13   I would not obey my teachers
          or turn my ear to my instructors.
14   And I was soon in serious trouble
          in the assembly of God's people."

15   Drink water from your own cistern,
          running water from your own well.
16   Should your springs overflow in the streets,
          your streams of water in the public squares?
17   Let them be yours alone,
          never to be shared with strangers.
18   May your fountain be blessed,
          and may you rejoice in the wife of your
              youth.
19   A loving doe, a graceful deer —
          may her breasts satisfy you always,
          may you ever be intoxicated with her love.
20   Why, my son, be intoxicated with another
              man's wife?
          Why embrace the bosom of a wayward
              woman?

21   For your ways are in full view of the LORD,
          and he examines all your paths.
22   The evil deeds of the wicked ensnare them;
          the cords of their sins hold them fast.
23   For lack of discipline they will die,
          led astray by their own great folly.

PROVERBS 6

Warnings Against Folly

1   My son, if you have put up security for your
        neighbor,
            if you have shaken hands in pledge for a
            stranger,
2   you have been trapped by what you said,
        ensnared by the words of your mouth.
3   So do this, my son, to free yourself,
        since you have fallen into your neighbor's
            hands:
    Go — to the point of exhaustion —
        and give your neighbor no rest!
4   Allow no sleep to your eyes,
        no slumber to your eyelids.
5   Free yourself, like a gazelle from the hand
            of the hunter,
        like a bird from the snare of the fowler.

6   Go to the ant, you sluggard;
        consider its ways and be wise!
7   It has no commander,
        no overseer or ruler,
8   yet it stores its provisions in summer
        and gathers its food at harvest.

9   How long will you lie there, you sluggard?
        When will you get up from your
            sleep?

10	A little sleep, a little slumber,
	a little folding of the hands to rest —
11	and poverty will come on you like a thief
	and scarcity like an armed man.

12	A troublemaker and a villain,
	who goes about with a corrupt mouth,
13	who winks maliciously with his eye,
	signals with his feet
	and motions with his fingers,
14	who plots evil with deceit in his heart —
	he always stirs up conflict.
15	Therefore disaster will overtake him in an
	instant;
	he will suddenly be destroyed — without
	remedy.

16	There are six things the LORD hates,
	seven that are detestable to him:
17	haughty eyes,
	a lying tongue,
	hands that shed innocent blood,
18	a heart that devises wicked schemes,
	feet that are quick to rush into evil,
19	a false witness who pours out lies
	and a person who stirs up conflict in the
	community.

Warning Against Adultery

20	My son, keep your father's command
	and do not forsake your mother's teaching.
21	Bind them always on your heart;
	fasten them around your neck.

22 When you walk, they will guide you;
  when you sleep, they will watch over you;
  when you awake, they will speak to you.
23 For this command is a lamp,
  this teaching is a light,
  and correction and instruction
  are the way to life,
24 keeping you from your neighbor's wife,
  from the smooth talk of a wayward woman.

25 Do not lust in your heart after her beauty
  or let her captivate you with her eyes.

26 For a prostitute can be had for a loaf of bread,
  but another man's wife preys on your very
    life.
27 Can a man scoop fire into his lap
  without his clothes being burned?
28 Can a man walk on hot coals
  without his feet being scorched?
29 So is he who sleeps with another man's wife;
  no one who touches her will go unpunished.

30 People do not despise a thief if he steals
  to satisfy his hunger when he is starving.
31 Yet if he is caught, he must pay sevenfold,
  though it costs him all the wealth of his
    house.
32 But a man who commits adultery has no
    sense;
  whoever does so destroys himself.
33 Blows and disgrace are his lot,
  and his shame will never be wiped away.

34 For jealousy arouses a husband's fury,
and he will show no mercy when he takes
revenge.
35 He will not accept any compensation;
he will refuse a bribe, however great it is.

PROVERBS 7

Warning Against the Adulterous Woman

1   My son, keep my words
         and store up my commands within you.
2   Keep my commands and you will live;
         guard my teachings as the apple of your eye.
3   Bind them on your fingers;
         write them on the tablet of your heart.
4   Say to wisdom, "You are my sister,"
         and to insight, "You are my relative."
5   They will keep you from the adulterous
              woman,
         from the wayward woman with her
              seductive words.

6   At the window of my house
         I looked down through the lattice.
7   I saw among the simple,
         I noticed among the young men,
         a youth who had no sense.
8   He was going down the street near her
              corner,
         walking along in the direction of her house
9   at twilight, as the day was fading,
         as the dark of night set in.

10   Then out came a woman to meet him,
         dressed like a prostitute and with crafty
              intent.

11 (She is unruly and defiant,
    her feet never stay at home;
12 now in the street, now in the squares,
    at every corner she lurks.)
13 She took hold of him and kissed him
    and with a brazen face she said:

14 "Today I fulfilled my vows,
    and I have food from my fellowship
        offering at home.
15 So I came out to meet you;
    I looked for you and have found you!
16 I have covered my bed
    with colored linens from Egypt.
17 I have perfumed my bed
    with myrrh, aloes and cinnamon.
18 Come, let's drink deeply of love till morning;
    let's enjoy ourselves with love!
19 My husband is not at home;
    he has gone on a long journey.
20 He took his purse filled with money
    and will not be home till full moon."

21 With persuasive words she led him
      astray;
    she seduced him with her smooth talk.
22 All at once he followed her
    like an ox going to the slaughter,
like a deer stepping into a noose
23   till an arrow pierces his liver,
like a bird darting into a snare,
    little knowing it will cost him his life.

24   Now then, my sons, listen to me;
          pay attention to what I say.
25   Do not let your heart turn to her ways
          or stray into her paths.
26   Many are the victims she has brought down;
          her slain are a mighty throng.
27   Her house is a highway to the grave,
          leading down to the chambers of death.

PROVERBS 8

Wisdom's Call

1   Does not wisdom call out?
      Does not understanding raise her voice?

2   At the highest point along the way,
      where the paths meet, she takes her stand;

3   beside the gate leading into the city,
      at the entrance, she cries aloud:

4   "To you, O people, I call out;
      I raise my voice to all mankind.

5   You who are simple, gain prudence;
      you who are foolish, set your hearts on it.

6   Listen, for I have trustworthy things to say;
      I open my lips to speak what is right.

7   My mouth speaks what is true,
      for my lips detest wickedness.

8   All the words of my mouth are just;
      none of them is crooked or perverse.

9   To the discerning all of them are right;
      they are upright to those who have found
        knowledge.

10   Choose my instruction instead of silver,
      knowledge rather than choice gold,

11   for wisdom is more precious than rubies,
      and nothing you desire can compare with her.

12   "I, wisdom, dwell together with prudence;
      I possess knowledge and discretion.

13 To fear the LORD is to hate evil;
    I hate pride and arrogance,
      evil behavior and perverse speech.
14 Counsel and sound judgment are
      mine;
    I have insight, I have power.
15 By me kings reign
    and rulers issue decrees that are just;
16 by me princes govern,
    and nobles — all who rule on earth.
17 I love those who love me,
    and those who seek me find me.
18 With me are riches and honor,
    enduring wealth and prosperity.
19 My fruit is better than fine gold;
    what I yield surpasses choice silver.
20 I walk in the way of righteousness,
    along the paths of justice,
21 bestowing a rich inheritance on those who
      love me
    and making their treasuries full.

22 "The LORD brought me forth as the first
      of his works,
    before his deeds of old;
23 I was formed long ages ago,
    at the very beginning, when the world
      came to be.
24 When there were no watery depths, I was
      given birth,
    when there were no springs overflowing
      with water;

25 before the mountains were settled in place,
    before the hills, I was given birth,
26 before he made the world or its fields
    or any of the dust of the earth.
27 I was there when he set the heavens in place,
    when he marked out the horizon on the face
      of the deep,
28 when he established the clouds above
    and fixed securely the fountains of the deep,
29 when he gave the sea its boundary
    so the waters would not overstep his
      command,
    and when he marked out the foundations of
      the earth.
30   Then I was constantly at his side.
    I was filled with delight day after day,
      rejoicing always in his presence,
31   rejoicing in his whole world
      and delighting in mankind.

32 "Now then, my children, listen to me;
    blessed are those who keep my ways.
33 Listen to my instruction and be wise;
    do not disregard it.
34 Blessed are those who listen to me,
    watching daily at my doors,
    waiting at my doorway.
35 For those who find me find life
    and receive favor from the LORD.
36 But those who fail to find me harm
      themselves;
    all who hate me love death."

PROVERBS 9

Invitations of Wisdom and Folly

1   Wisdom has built her house;
>   she has set up its seven pillars.
2   She has prepared her meat and mixed her
>   wine;
>   she has also set her table.
3   She has sent out her servants, and she calls
>   from the highest point of the city,
4   "Let all who are simple come to my
>   house!"
>   To those who have no sense she says,
5   "Come, eat my food
>   and drink the wine I have mixed.
6   Leave your simple ways and you will live;
>   walk in the way of insight."

7   Whoever corrects a mocker invites insults;
>   whoever rebukes the wicked incurs abuse.
8   Do not rebuke mockers or they will hate you;
>   rebuke the wise and they will love you.
9   Instruct the wise and they will be wiser still;
>   teach the righteous and they will add to
>   their learning.

10   The fear of the LORD is the beginning of
>   wisdom,
>   and knowledge of the Holy One is
>   understanding.

11   For through wisdom your days will be many,
          and years will be added to your life.
12   If you are wise, your wisdom will reward you;
          if you are a mocker, you alone will suffer.

13   Folly is an unruly woman;
          she is simple and knows nothing.
14   She sits at the door of her house,
          on a seat at the highest point of the city,
15   calling out to those who pass by,
          who go straight on their way,
16   "Let all who are simple come to my house!"
      To those who have no sense she says,
17   "Stolen water is sweet;
          food eaten in secret is delicious!"
18   But little do they know that the dead are there,
          that her guests are deep in the realm of the
              dead.

PROVERBS 10

1 The proverbs of Solomon:

A wise son brings joy to his father,
     but a foolish son brings grief to his mother.

2 Ill-gotten treasures have no lasting value,
     but righteousness delivers from death.

3 The LORD does not let the righteous go hungry,
     but he thwarts the craving of the wicked.

4 Lazy hands make for poverty,
     but diligent hands bring wealth.

5 He who gathers crops in summer is a prudent
     son,
     but he who sleeps during harvest is a
     disgraceful son.

6 Blessings crown the head of the righteous,
     but violence overwhelms the mouth of the
     wicked.

7 The name of the righteous is used in
     blessings,
     but the name of the wicked will rot.

8 The wise in heart accept commands,
     but a chattering fool comes to ruin.

9   Whoever walks in integrity walks securely,
         but whoever takes crooked paths will be
             found out.

10   Whoever winks maliciously causes grief,
         and a chattering fool comes to ruin.

11   The mouth of the righteous is a fountain
             of life,
         but the mouth of the wicked conceals
             violence.

12   Hatred stirs up conflict,
         but love covers over all wrongs.

13   Wisdom is found on the lips of the discerning,
         but a rod is for the back of one who has
             no sense.

14   The wise store up knowledge,
         but the mouth of a fool invites ruin.

15   The wealth of the rich is their fortified city,
         but poverty is the ruin of the poor.

16   The wages of the righteous is life,
         but the earnings of the wicked are sin and
             death.

17   Whoever heeds discipline shows the way to life,
         but whoever ignores correction leads others
             astray.

18   Whoever conceals hatred with lying lips
         and spreads slander is a fool.

19   Sin is not ended by multiplying words,
            but the prudent hold their tongues.

20   The tongue of the righteous is choice silver,
            but the heart of the wicked is of little value.

21   The lips of the righteous nourish many,
            but fools die for lack of sense.

22   The blessing of the LORD brings wealth,
            without painful toil for it.

23   A fool finds pleasure in wicked schemes,
            but a person of understanding delights in
                wisdom.

24   What the wicked dread will overtake them;
            what the righteous desire will be granted.

25   When the storm has swept by, the wicked are
                gone,
            but the righteous stand firm forever.

26   As vinegar to the teeth and smoke to the eyes,
            so are sluggards to those who send them.

27   The fear of the LORD adds length to life,
            but the years of the wicked are cut short.

28   The prospect of the righteous is joy,
            but the hopes of the wicked come to
                nothing.

29   The way of the LORD is a refuge for the
                blameless,
            but it is the ruin of those who do evil.

30   The righteous will never be uprooted,
         but the wicked will not remain in the land.

31   From the mouth of the righteous comes the
            fruit of wisdom,
         but a perverse tongue will be silenced.

32   The lips of the righteous know what finds
            favor,
         but the mouth of the wicked only what is
            perverse.

PROVERBS 11

1   The LORD detests dishonest scales,
      but accurate weights find favor with
        him.

2   When pride comes, then comes disgrace,
      but with humility comes wisdom.

3   The integrity of the upright guides them,
      but the unfaithful are destroyed by their
        duplicity.

4   Wealth is worthless in the day of wrath,
      but righteousness delivers from death.

5   The righteousness of the blameless makes
        their paths straight,
      but the wicked are brought down by their
        own wickedness.

6   The righteousness of the upright delivers
        them,
      but the unfaithful are trapped by evil
        desires.

7   Hopes placed in mortals die with them;
      all the promise of their power comes to
        nothing.

8   The righteous person is rescued from
        trouble,
      and it falls on the wicked instead.

9   With their mouths the godless destroy their
           neighbors,
        but through knowledge the righteous
           escape.

10   When the righteous prosper, the city rejoices;
        when the wicked perish, there are shouts
           of joy.

11   Through the blessing of the upright a city is
           exalted,
        but by the mouth of the wicked it is
           destroyed.

12   Whoever derides their neighbor has no
           sense,
        but the one who has understanding holds
           their tongue.

13   A gossip betrays a confidence,
        but a trustworthy person keeps a secret.

14   For lack of guidance a nation falls,
        but victory is won through many advisers.

15   Whoever puts up security for a stranger will
           surely suffer,
        but whoever refuses to shake hands in
           pledge is safe.

16   A kindhearted woman gains honor,
        but ruthless men gain only wealth.

17   Those who are kind benefit themselves,
        but the cruel bring ruin on themselves.

18   A wicked person earns deceptive wages,
       but the one who sows righteousness reaps a
         sure reward.

19   Truly the righteous attain life,
       but whoever pursues evil finds death.

20   The Lord detests those whose hearts are
         perverse,
       but he delights in those whose ways are
         blameless.

21   Be sure of this: The wicked will not go
         unpunished,
       but those who are righteous will go free.

22   Like a gold ring in a pig's snout
       is a beautiful woman who shows no
         discretion.

23   The desire of the righteous ends only in good,
       but the hope of the wicked only in wrath.

24   One person gives freely, yet gains even more;
       another withholds unduly, but comes to
         poverty.

25   A generous person will prosper;
       whoever refreshes others will be refreshed.

26   People curse the one who hoards grain,
       but they pray God's blessing on the one who
         is willing to sell.

27   Whoever seeks good finds favor,
       but evil comes to one who searches for it.

28   Those who trust in their riches will fall,
       but the righteous will thrive like a green
           leaf.

29   Whoever brings ruin on their family will
           inherit only wind,
       and the fool will be servant to the wise.

30   The fruit of the righteous is a tree of life,
       and the one who is wise saves lives.

31   If the righteous receive their due on earth,
       how much more the ungodly and the sinner!

PROVERBS 12

1   Whoever loves discipline loves knowledge,
       but whoever hates correction is stupid.

2   Good people obtain favor from the Lord,
       but he condemns those who devise wicked
          schemes.

3   No one can be established through wickedness,
       but the righteous cannot be uprooted.

4   A wife of noble character is her husband's
          crown,
       but a disgraceful wife is like decay in his
          bones.

5   The plans of the righteous are just,
       but the advice of the wicked is deceitful.

6   The words of the wicked lie in wait for blood,
       but the speech of the upright rescues them.

7   The wicked are overthrown and are no more,
       but the house of the righteous stands firm.

8   A person is praised according to their
          prudence,
       and one with a warped mind is despised.

9   Better to be a nobody and yet have a servant
       than pretend to be somebody and have no
          food.

10   The righteous care for the needs of their
           animals,
         but the kindest acts of the wicked are cruel.

11   Those who work their land will have abundant
           food,
         but those who chase fantasies have no sense.

12   The wicked desire the stronghold of evildoers,
         but the root of the righteous endures.

13   Evildoers are trapped by their sinful talk,
         and so the innocent escape trouble.

14   From the fruit of their lips people are filled
           with good things,
         and the work of their hands brings them
           reward.

15   The way of fools seems right to them,
         but the wise listen to advice.

16   Fools show their annoyance at once,
         but the prudent overlook an insult.

17   An honest witness tells the truth,
         but a false witness tells lies.

18   The words of the reckless pierce like swords,
         but the tongue of the wise brings healing.

19   Truthful lips endure forever,
         but a lying tongue lasts only a moment.

20   Deceit is in the hearts of those who plot evil,
         but those who promote peace have joy.

21 No harm overtakes the righteous,
       but the wicked have their fill of trouble.

22 The Lord detests lying lips,
       but he delights in people who are
           trustworthy.

23 The prudent keep their knowledge to
       themselves,
       but a fool's heart blurts out folly.

24 Diligent hands will rule,
       but laziness ends in forced labor.

25 Anxiety weighs down the heart,
       but a kind word cheers it up.

26 The righteous choose their friends carefully,
       but the way of the wicked leads them astray.

27 The lazy do not roast any game,
       but the diligent feed on the riches of the
           hunt.

28 In the way of righteousness there is life;
       along that path is immortality.

PROVERBS 13

1   A wise son heeds his father's instruction,
       but a mocker does not respond to rebukes.

2   From the fruit of their lips people enjoy good
          things,
       but the unfaithful have an appetite for
          violence.

3   Those who guard their lips preserve their lives,
       but those who speak rashly will come to
          ruin.

4   A sluggard's appetite is never filled,
       but the desires of the diligent are fully
          satisfied.

5   The righteous hate what is false,
       but the wicked make themselves a stench
       and bring shame on themselves.

6   Righteousness guards the person of integrity,
       but wickedness overthrows the sinner.

7   One person pretends to be rich, yet has
          nothing;
       another pretends to be poor, yet has great
          wealth.

8   A person's riches may ransom their life,
       but the poor cannot respond to threatening
          rebukes.

9   The light of the righteous shines brightly,
        but the lamp of the wicked is snuffed out.

10 Where there is strife, there is pride,
        but wisdom is found in those who take
            advice.

11 Dishonest money dwindles away,
        but whoever gathers money little by little
            makes it grow.

12 Hope deferred makes the heart sick,
        but a longing fulfilled is a tree of life.

13 Whoever scorns instruction will pay for it,
        but whoever respects a command is
            rewarded.

14 The teaching of the wise is a fountain
        of life,
        turning a person from the snares of
            death.

15 Good judgment wins favor,
        but the way of the unfaithful leads to their
            destruction.

16 All who are prudent act with knowledge,
        but fools expose their folly.

17 A wicked messenger falls into trouble,
        but a trustworthy envoy brings healing.

18 Whoever disregards discipline comes to
            poverty and shame,
        but whoever heeds correction is honored.

19 A longing fulfilled is sweet to the soul,
   but fools detest turning from evil.

20 Walk with the wise and become wise,
   for a companion of fools suffers harm.

21 Trouble pursues the sinner,
   but the righteous are rewarded with good
   things.

22 A good person leaves an inheritance for their
   children's children,
   but a sinner's wealth is stored up for the
   righteous.

23 An unplowed field produces food for the poor,
   but injustice sweeps it away.

24 Whoever spares the rod hates their children,
   but the one who loves their children is
   careful to discipline them.

25 The righteous eat to their hearts' content,
   but the stomach of the wicked goes hungry.

PROVERBS 14

1   The wise woman builds her house,
    but with her own hands the foolish one tears
        hers down.

2   Whoever fears the LORD walks uprightly,
    but those who despise him are devious in
        their ways.

3   A fool's mouth lashes out with pride,
    but the lips of the wise protect them.

4   Where there are no oxen, the manger is empty,
    but from the strength of an ox come
        abundant harvests.

5   An honest witness does not deceive,
    but a false witness pours out lies.

6   The mocker seeks wisdom and finds none,
    but knowledge comes easily to the
        discerning.

7   Stay away from a fool,
    for you will not find knowledge on their lips.

8   The wisdom of the prudent is to give thought
        to their ways,
    but the folly of fools is deception.

9   Fools mock at making amends for sin,
    but goodwill is found among the upright.

10   Each heart knows its own bitterness,
         and no one else can share its joy.

11   The house of the wicked will be destroyed,
         but the tent of the upright will flourish.

12   There is a way that appears to be right,
         but in the end it leads to death.

13   Even in laughter the heart may ache,
         and rejoicing may end in grief.

14   The faithless will be fully repaid for their ways,
         and the good rewarded for theirs.

15   The simple believe anything,
         but the prudent give thought to their
             steps.

16   The wise fear the LORD and shun evil,
         but a fool is hotheaded and yet feels secure.

17   A quick-tempered person does foolish things,
         and the one who devises evil schemes is
             hated.

18   The simple inherit folly,
         but the prudent are crowned with
             knowledge.

19   Evildoers will bow down in the presence of the
             good,
         and the wicked at the gates of the righteous.

20   The poor are shunned even by their neighbors,
         but the rich have many friends.

21 It is a sin to despise one's neighbor,
   but blessed is the one who is kind to the
      needy.

22 Do not those who plot evil go astray?
   But those who plan what is good find love
      and faithfulness.

23 All hard work brings a profit,
   but mere talk leads only to poverty.

24 The wealth of the wise is their crown,
   but the folly of fools yields folly.

25 A truthful witness saves lives,
   but a false witness is deceitful.

26 Whoever fears the LORD has a secure fortress,
   and for their children it will be a refuge.

27 The fear of the LORD is a fountain of life,
   turning a person from the snares of death.

28 A large population is a king's glory,
   but without subjects a prince is ruined.

29 Whoever is patient has great understanding,
   but one who is quick-tempered displays
      folly.

30 A heart at peace gives life to the body,
   but envy rots the bones.

31 Whoever oppresses the poor shows contempt
      for their Maker,
   but whoever is kind to the needy honors
      God.

32   When calamity comes, the wicked are brought
             down,
         but even in death the righteous seek refuge
             in God.

33   Wisdom reposes in the heart of the discerning
         and even among fools she lets herself be
             known.

34   Righteousness exalts a nation,
         but sin condemns any people.

35   A king delights in a wise servant,
         but a shameful servant arouses his fury.

PROVERBS 15

1   A gentle answer turns away wrath,
      but a harsh word stirs up anger.

2   The tongue of the wise adorns knowledge,
      but the mouth of the fool gushes folly.

3   The eyes of the Lord are everywhere,
      keeping watch on the wicked and the
        good.

4   The soothing tongue is a tree of life,
      but a perverse tongue crushes the spirit.

5   A fool spurns a parent's discipline,
      but whoever heeds correction shows
        prudence.

6   The house of the righteous contains great
        treasure,
      but the income of the wicked brings ruin.

7   The lips of the wise spread knowledge,
      but the hearts of fools are not upright.

8   The Lord detests the sacrifice of the wicked,
      but the prayer of the upright pleases
        him.

9   The Lord detests the way of the wicked,
      but he loves those who pursue
        righteousness.

10   Stern discipline awaits anyone who leaves
            the path;
        the one who hates correction will die.

11   Death and Destruction lie open before the
            LORD —
        how much more do human hearts!

12   Mockers resent correction,
        so they avoid the wise.

13   A happy heart makes the face cheerful,
        but heartache crushes the spirit.

14   The discerning heart seeks knowledge,
        but the mouth of a fool feeds on folly.

15   All the days of the oppressed are wretched,
        but the cheerful heart has a continual
            feast.

16   Better a little with the fear of the LORD
        than great wealth with turmoil.

17   Better a small serving of vegetables with love
        than a fattened calf with hatred.

18   A hot-tempered person stirs up conflict,
        but the one who is patient calms a quarrel.

19   The way of the sluggard is blocked with
            thorns,
        but the path of the upright is a highway.

20   A wise son brings joy to his father,
        but a foolish man despises his mother.

21 Folly brings joy to one who has no sense,
    but whoever has understanding keeps a
        straight course.

22 Plans fail for lack of counsel,
    but with many advisers they succeed.

23 A person finds joy in giving an apt reply —
    and how good is a timely word!

24 The path of life leads upward for the prudent
    to keep them from going down to the realm
        of the dead.

25 The LORD tears down the house of the proud,
    but he sets the widow's boundary stones in
        place.

26 The LORD detests the thoughts of the wicked,
    but gracious words are pure in his sight.

27 The greedy bring ruin to their households,
    but the one who hates bribes will live.

28 The heart of the righteous weighs its answers,
    but the mouth of the wicked gushes evil.

29 The LORD is far from the wicked,
    but he hears the prayer of the righteous.

30 Light in a messenger's eyes brings joy to the
        heart,
    and good news gives health to the bones.

31 Whoever heeds life-giving correction
    will be at home among the wise.

32 Those who disregard discipline despise
themselves,
but the one who heeds correction gains
understanding.

33 Wisdom's instruction is to fear the LORD,
and humility comes before honor.

PROVERBS 16

1   To humans belong the plans of the heart,
      but from the LORD comes the proper answer
         of the tongue.

2   All a person's ways seem pure to them,
      but motives are weighed by the LORD.

3   Commit to the LORD whatever you do,
      and he will establish your plans.

4   The LORD works out everything to its proper
         end —
      even the wicked for a day of disaster.

5   The LORD detests all the proud of heart.
      Be sure of this: They will not go unpunished.

6   Through love and faithfulness sin is atoned
         for;
      through the fear of the LORD evil is avoided.

7   When the LORD takes pleasure in anyone's
         way,
      he causes their enemies to make peace
         with them.

8   Better a little with righteousness
      than much gain with injustice.

9   In their hearts humans plan their course,
      but the LORD establishes their steps.

10   The lips of a king speak as an oracle,
       and his mouth does not betray justice.

11   Honest scales and balances belong to the LORD;
       all the weights in the bag are of his making.

12   Kings detest wrongdoing,
       for a throne is established through
         righteousness.

13   Kings take pleasure in honest lips;
       they value the one who speaks what is right.

14   A king's wrath is a messenger of death,
       but the wise will appease it.

15   When a king's face brightens, it means life;
       his favor is like a rain cloud in spring.

16   How much better to get wisdom than gold,
       to get insight rather than silver!

17   The highway of the upright avoids evil;
       those who guard their ways preserve their
        lives.

18   Pride goes before destruction,
       a haughty spirit before a fall.

19   Better to be lowly in spirit along with the
        oppressed
       than to share plunder with the proud.

20   Whoever gives heed to instruction prospers,
       and blessed is the one who trusts in the
        LORD.

21 The wise in heart are called discerning,
and gracious words promote instruction.

22 Prudence is a fountain of life to the prudent,
but folly brings punishment to fools.

23 The hearts of the wise make their mouths
prudent,
and their lips promote instruction.

24 Gracious words are a honeycomb,
sweet to the soul and healing to the
bones.

25 There is a way that appears to be right,
but in the end it leads to death.

26 The appetite of laborers works for them;
their hunger drives them on.

27 A scoundrel plots evil,
and on their lips it is like a scorching fire.

28 A perverse person stirs up conflict,
and a gossip separates close friends.

29 A violent person entices their neighbor
and leads them down a path that is not
good.

30 Whoever winks with their eye is plotting
perversity;
whoever purses their lips is bent on evil.

31 Gray hair is a crown of splendor;
it is attained in the way of righteousness.

32   Better a patient person than a warrior,
         one with self-control than one who takes
            a city.

33   The lot is cast into the lap,
         but its every decision is from the LORD.

PROVERBS 17

1   Better a dry crust with peace and quiet
    than a house full of feasting, with strife.

2   A prudent servant will rule over a disgraceful
        son
    and will share the inheritance as one of the
        family.

3   The crucible for silver and the furnace for
        gold,
    but the Lord tests the heart.

4   A wicked person listens to deceitful lips;
    a liar pays attention to a destructive
        tongue.

5   Whoever mocks the poor shows contempt for
        their Maker;
    whoever gloats over disaster will not go
        unpunished.

6   Children's children are a crown to the aged,
    and parents are the pride of their children.

7   Eloquent lips are unsuited to a godless
        fool —
    how much worse lying lips to a ruler!

8   A bribe is seen as a charm by the one who
        gives it;
    they think success will come at every turn.

9   Whoever would foster love covers over an
         offense,
             but whoever repeats the matter separates
                 close friends.

10   A rebuke impresses a discerning person
         more than a hundred lashes a fool.

11   Evildoers foster rebellion against God;
         the messenger of death will be sent against
             them.

12   Better to meet a bear robbed of her cubs
         than a fool bent on folly.

13   Evil will never leave the house
         of one who pays back evil for good.

14   Starting a quarrel is like breaching a dam;
         so drop the matter before a dispute breaks
             out.

15   Acquitting the guilty and condemning the
         innocent —
             the LORD detests them both.

16   Why should fools have money in hand to
         buy wisdom,
             when they are not able to understand it?

17   A friend loves at all times,
         and a brother is born for a time of
             adversity.

18   One who has no sense shakes hands in pledge
         and puts up security for a neighbor.

19   Whoever loves a quarrel loves sin;
          whoever builds a high gate invites
              destruction.

20   One whose heart is corrupt does not prosper;
          one whose tongue is perverse falls into
              trouble.

21   To have a fool for a child brings grief;
          there is no joy for the parent of a godless
              fool.

22   A cheerful heart is good medicine,
          but a crushed spirit dries up the bones.

23   The wicked accept bribes in secret
          to pervert the course of justice.

24   A discerning person keeps wisdom in view,
          but a fool's eyes wander to the ends of the
              earth.

25   A foolish son brings grief to his father
          and bitterness to the mother who bore him.

26   If imposing a fine on the innocent is not good,
          surely to flog honest officials is not right.

27   The one who has knowledge uses words with
              restraint,
          and whoever has understanding is even-
              tempered.

28   Even fools are thought wise if they keep
              silent,
          and discerning if they hold their tongues.

PROVERBS 18

1   An unfriendly person pursues selfish ends
        and against all sound judgment starts
        quarrels.

2   Fools find no pleasure in understanding
        but delight in airing their own opinions.

3   When wickedness comes, so does contempt,
        and with shame comes reproach.

4   The words of the mouth are deep waters,
        but the fountain of wisdom is a rushing
        stream.

5   It is not good to be partial to the wicked
        and so deprive the innocent of justice.

6   The lips of fools bring them strife,
        and their mouths invite a beating.

7   The mouths of fools are their undoing,
        and their lips are a snare to their very
        lives.

8   The words of a gossip are like choice morsels;
        they go down to the inmost parts.

9   One who is slack in his work
        is brother to one who destroys.

10   The name of the LORD is a fortified tower;
        the righteous run to it and are safe.

11   The wealth of the rich is their fortified city;
         they imagine it a wall too high to scale.

12   Before a downfall the heart is haughty,
         but humility comes before honor.

13   To answer before listening —
         that is folly and shame.

14   The human spirit can endure in sickness,
         but a crushed spirit who can bear?

15   The heart of the discerning acquires
             knowledge,
         for the ears of the wise seek it out.

16   A gift opens the way
         and ushers the giver into the presence of the
             great.

17   In a lawsuit the first to speak seems right,
         until someone comes forward and cross-
             examines.

18   Casting the lot settles disputes
         and keeps strong opponents apart.

19   A brother wronged is more unyielding than a
             fortified city;
         disputes are like the barred gates of a
             citadel.

20   From the fruit of their mouth a person's
             stomach is filled;
         with the harvest of their lips they are
             satisfied.

21 The tongue has the power of life and death,
and those who love it will eat its fruit.

22 He who finds a wife finds what is good
and receives favor from the LORD.

23 The poor plead for mercy,
but the rich answer harshly.

24 One who has unreliable friends soon comes to
ruin,
but there is a friend who sticks closer than a
brother.

PROVERBS 19

1　　Better the poor whose walk is blameless
　　　than a fool whose lips are perverse.

2　　Desire without knowledge is not good —
　　　how much more will hasty feet miss the
　　　　way!

3　　A person's own folly leads to their ruin,
　　　yet their heart rages against the LORD.

4　　Wealth attracts many friends,
　　　but even the closest friend of the poor
　　　　person deserts them.

5　　A false witness will not go unpunished,
　　　and whoever pours out lies will not go
　　　　free.

6　　Many curry favor with a ruler,
　　　and everyone is the friend of one who gives
　　　　gifts.

7　　The poor are shunned by all their relatives —
　　　how much more do their friends avoid
　　　　them!
　　Though the poor pursue them with pleading,
　　　they are nowhere to be found.

8　　The one who gets wisdom loves life;
　　　the one who cherishes understanding will
　　　　soon prosper.

9   A false witness will not go unpunished,
        and whoever pours out lies will perish.

10   It is not fitting for a fool to live in luxury —
        how much worse for a slave to rule over
            princes!

11   A person's wisdom yields patience;
        it is to one's glory to overlook an offense.

12   A king's rage is like the roar of a lion,
        but his favor is like dew on the grass.

13   A foolish child is a father's ruin,
        and a quarrelsome wife is like
            the constant dripping of a leaky roof.

14   Houses and wealth are inherited from
            parents,
        but a prudent wife is from the LORD.

15   Laziness brings on deep sleep,
        and the shiftless go hungry.

16   Whoever keeps commandments keeps their
            life,
        but whoever shows contempt for their ways
            will die.

17   Whoever is kind to the poor lends to the LORD,
        and he will reward them for what they have
            done.

18   Discipline your children, for in that there is
            hope;
        do not be a willing party to their death.

19   A hot-tempered person must pay the penalty;
           rescue them, and you will have to do it
               again.

20   Listen to advice and accept discipline,
           and at the end you will be counted among
               the wise.

21   Many are the plans in a person's heart,
           but it is the LORD's purpose that prevails.

22   What a person desires is unfailing love;
           better to be poor than a liar.

23   The fear of the LORD leads to life;
           then one rests content, untouched by
               trouble.

24   A sluggard buries his hand in the dish;
           he will not even bring it back to his
               mouth!

25   Flog a mocker, and the simple will learn
               prudence;
           rebuke the discerning, and they will gain
               knowledge.

26   Whoever robs their father and drives out
               their mother
           is a child who brings shame and
               disgrace.

27   Stop listening to instruction, my son,
           and you will stray from the words of
               knowledge.

28 A corrupt witness mocks at justice,
        and the mouth of the wicked gulps
            down evil.

29 Penalties are prepared for mockers,
        and beatings for the backs of fools.

PROVERBS 20

1   Wine is a mocker and beer a brawler;
    whoever is led astray by them is not wise.

2   A king's wrath strikes terror like the roar of a
        lion;
    those who anger him forfeit their lives.

3   It is to one's honor to avoid strife,
    but every fool is quick to quarrel.

4   Sluggards do not plow in season;
    so at harvest time they look but find
        nothing.

5   The purposes of a person's heart are deep
        waters,
    but one who has insight draws them out.

6   Many claim to have unfailing love,
    but a faithful person who can find?

7   The righteous lead blameless lives;
    blessed are their children after them.

8   When a king sits on his throne to judge,
    he winnows out all evil with his eyes.

9   Who can say, "I have kept my heart pure;
    I am clean and without sin"?

10 Differing weights and differing measures —
    the LORD detests them both.

11 Even small children are known by their
            actions,
        so is their conduct really pure and upright?

12 Ears that hear and eyes that see —
        the LORD has made them both.

13 Do not love sleep or you will grow poor;
        stay awake and you will have food to spare.

14 "It's no good, it's no good!" says the buyer —
        then goes off and boasts about the purchase.

15 Gold there is, and rubies in abundance,
        but lips that speak knowledge are a rare
            jewel.

16 Take the garment of one who puts up security
            for a stranger;
        hold it in pledge if it is done for an outsider.

17 Food gained by fraud tastes sweet,
        but one ends up with a mouth full of gravel.

18 Plans are established by seeking advice;
        so if you wage war, obtain guidance.

19 A gossip betrays a confidence;
        so avoid anyone who talks too much.

20 If someone curses their father or mother,
        their lamp will be snuffed out in pitch
            darkness.

21 An inheritance claimed too soon
        will not be blessed at the end.

22 Do not say, "I'll pay you back for this wrong!"
        Wait for the LORD, and he will avenge you.

23 The LORD detests differing weights,
        and dishonest scales do not please him.

24 A person's steps are directed by the LORD.
        How then can anyone understand their
            own way?

25 It is a trap to dedicate something rashly
        and only later to consider one's vows.

26 A wise king winnows out the wicked;
        he drives the threshing wheel over them.

27 The human spirit is the lamp of the LORD
        that sheds light on one's inmost being.

28 Love and faithfulness keep a king safe;
        through love his throne is made secure.

29 The glory of young men is their strength,
        gray hair the splendor of the old.

30 Blows and wounds scrub away evil,
        and beatings purge the inmost being.

1   In the LORD's hand the king's heart is a stream
        of water
        that he channels toward all who please
        him.

2   A person may think their own ways are right,
        but the LORD weighs the heart.

3   To do what is right and just
        is more acceptable to the LORD than
        sacrifice.

4   Haughty eyes and a proud heart —
        the unplowed field of the wicked —
        produce sin.

5   The plans of the diligent lead to profit
        as surely as haste leads to poverty.

6   A fortune made by a lying tongue
        is a fleeting vapor and a deadly snare.

7   The violence of the wicked will drag them
        away,
        for they refuse to do what is right.

8   The way of the guilty is devious,
        but the conduct of the innocent is upright.

9   Better to live on a corner of the roof
        than share a house with a quarrelsome wife.

10 The wicked crave evil;
their neighbors get no mercy from them.

11 When a mocker is punished, the simple gain
wisdom;
by paying attention to the wise they get
knowledge.

12 The Righteous One takes note of the house of
the wicked
and brings the wicked to ruin.

13 Whoever shuts their ears to the cry of the poor
will also cry out and not be answered.

14 A gift given in secret soothes anger,
and a bribe concealed in the cloak pacifies
great wrath.

15 When justice is done, it brings joy to the
righteous
but terror to evildoers.

16 Whoever strays from the path of prudence
comes to rest in the company of the dead.

17 Whoever loves pleasure will become poor;
whoever loves wine and olive oil will never
be rich.

18 The wicked become a ransom for the righteous,
and the unfaithful for the upright.

19 Better to live in a desert
than with a quarrelsome and nagging
wife.

20 The wise store up choice food and olive oil,
        but fools gulp theirs down.

21 Whoever pursues righteousness and love
        finds life, prosperity and honor.

22 One who is wise can go up against the city of
            the mighty
        and pull down the stronghold in which they
            trust.

23 Those who guard their mouths and their
            tongues
        keep themselves from calamity.

24 The proud and arrogant person — "Mocker" is
            his name —
        behaves with insolent fury.

25 The craving of a sluggard will be the death of
            him,
        because his hands refuse to work.
26 All day long he craves for more,
        but the righteous give without sparing.

27 The sacrifice of the wicked is detestable —
        how much more so when brought with evil
            intent!

28 A false witness will perish,
        but a careful listener will testify successfully.

29 The wicked put up a bold front,
        but the upright give thought to their
            ways.

30   There is no wisdom, no insight, no plan
         that can succeed against the LORD.

31   The horse is made ready for the day of battle,
         but victory rests with the LORD.

PROVERBS 22

1   A good name is more desirable than great
       riches;
     to be esteemed is better than silver or gold.

2   Rich and poor have this in common:
     The LORD is the Maker of them all.

3   The prudent see danger and take refuge,
     but the simple keep going and pay the
       penalty.

4   Humility is the fear of the LORD;
     its wages are riches and honor and life.

5   In the paths of the wicked are snares and
       pitfalls,
     but those who would preserve their life stay
       far from them.

6   Start children off on the way they should go,
     and even when they are old they will not
       turn from it.

7   The rich rule over the poor,
     and the borrower is slave to the lender.

8   Whoever sows injustice reaps calamity,
     and the rod they wield in fury will be broken.

9   The generous will themselves be blessed,
     for they share their food with the poor.

10   Drive out the mocker, and out goes strife;
         quarrels and insults are ended.

11   One who loves a pure heart and who speaks
             with grace
         will have the king for a friend.

12   The eyes of the LORD keep watch over
             knowledge,
         but he frustrates the words of the
             unfaithful.

13   The sluggard says, "There's a lion outside!
         I'll be killed in the public square!"

14   The mouth of an adulterous woman is a deep
             pit;
         a man who is under the LORD's wrath falls
             into it.

15   Folly is bound up in the heart of a child,
         but the rod of discipline will drive it far
             away.

16   One who oppresses the poor to increase his
             wealth
         and one who gives gifts to the rich — both
             come to poverty.

THIRTY SAYINGS OF THE WISE

SAYING 1

17   Pay attention and turn your ear to the sayings
             of the wise;
         apply your heart to what I teach,

18   for it is pleasing when you keep them in
             your heart
           and have all of them ready on your lips.
19   So that your trust may be in the LORD,
           I teach you today, even you.
20   Have I not written thirty sayings for you,
           sayings of counsel and knowledge,
21   teaching you to be honest and to speak the
             truth,
           so that you bring back truthful reports
           to those you serve?

SAYING 2

22   Do not exploit the poor because they are
             poor
           and do not crush the needy in court,
23   for the LORD will take up their case
           and will exact life for life.

SAYING 3

24   Do not make friends with a hot-tempered
             person,
           do not associate with one easily angered,
25   or you may learn their ways
           and get yourself ensnared.

SAYING 4

26   Do not be one who shakes hands in pledge
           or puts up security for debts;
27   if you lack the means to pay,
           your very bed will be snatched from under
             you.

SAYING 5

28 Do not move an ancient boundary stone
set up by your ancestors.

SAYING 6

29 Do you see someone skilled in their work?
They will serve before kings;
they will not serve before officials of low
rank.

PROVERBS 23

SAYING 7

1   When you sit to dine with a ruler,
      note well what is before you,
2   and put a knife to your throat
      if you are given to gluttony.
3   Do not crave his delicacies,
      for that food is deceptive.

SAYING 8

4   Do not wear yourself out to get rich;
      do not trust your own cleverness.
5   Cast but a glance at riches, and they are gone,
      for they will surely sprout wings
        and fly off to the sky like an eagle.

SAYING 9

6   Do not eat the food of a begrudging host,
      do not crave his delicacies;
7   for he is the kind of person
      who is always thinking about the cost.
    "Eat and drink," he says to you,
      but his heart is not with you.
8   You will vomit up the little you have eaten
      and will have wasted your compliments.

SAYING 10

9   Do not speak to fools,
      for they will scorn your prudent words.

SAYING 11

10   Do not move an ancient boundary stone
           or encroach on the fields of the fatherless,
11   for their Defender is strong;
           he will take up their case against you.

SAYING 12

12   Apply your heart to instruction
           and your ears to words of knowledge.

SAYING 13

13   Do not withhold discipline from a child;
           if you punish them with the rod, they will
               not die.
14   Punish them with the rod
           and save them from death.

SAYING 14

15   My son, if your heart is wise,
           then my heart will be glad indeed;
16   my inmost being will rejoice
           when your lips speak what is right.

SAYING 15

17   Do not let your heart envy sinners,
           but always be zealous for the fear of the
               LORD.
18   There is surely a future hope for you,
           and your hope will not be cut off.

SAYING 16

19   Listen, my son, and be wise,
           and set your heart on the right path:

20   Do not join those who drink too much wine
        or gorge themselves on meat,
21   for drunkards and gluttons become poor,
        and drowsiness clothes them in rags.

SAYING 17

22   Listen to your father, who gave you life,
        and do not despise your mother when she is
           old.
23   Buy the truth and do not sell it —
        wisdom, instruction and insight as well.
24   The father of a righteous child has great joy;
        a man who fathers a wise son rejoices in
           him.
25   May your father and mother rejoice;
        may she who gave you birth be joyful!

SAYING 18

26   My son, give me your heart
        and let your eyes delight in my ways,
27   for an adulterous woman is a deep pit,
        and a wayward wife is a narrow well.
28   Like a bandit she lies in wait
        and multiplies the unfaithful among men.

SAYING 19

29   Who has woe? Who has sorrow?
        Who has strife? Who has complaints?
        Who has needless bruises? Who has
           bloodshot eyes?
30   Those who linger over wine,
        who go to sample bowls of mixed wine.

31   Do not gaze at wine when it is red,
          when it sparkles in the cup,
          when it goes down smoothly!
32   In the end it bites like a snake
          and poisons like a viper.
33   Your eyes will see strange sights,
          and your mind will imagine confusing
              things.
34   You will be like one sleeping on the high seas,
          lying on top of the rigging.
35   "They hit me," you will say, "but I'm not hurt!
          They beat me, but I don't feel it!
      When will I wake up
          so I can find another drink?"

PROVERBS 24

SAYING 20

1 Do not envy the wicked,
    do not desire their company;
2 for their hearts plot violence,
    and their lips talk about making trouble.

SAYING 21

3 By wisdom a house is built,
    and through understanding it is established;
4 through knowledge its rooms are filled
    with rare and beautiful treasures.

SAYING 22

5 The wise prevail through great power,
    and those who have knowledge muster their
        strength.
6 Surely you need guidance to wage war,
    and victory is won through many advisers.

SAYING 23

7 Wisdom is too high for fools;
    in the assembly at the gate they must not
        open their mouths.

SAYING 24

8 Whoever plots evil
    will be known as a schemer.
9 The schemes of folly are sin,
    and people detest a mocker.

10 If you falter in a time of trouble,
    how small is your strength!
11 Rescue those being led away to death;
    hold back those staggering toward
        slaughter.
12 If you say, "But we knew nothing about this,"
    does not he who weighs the heart
        perceive it?
    Does not he who guards your life know it?
    Will he not repay everyone according to
        what they have done?

SAYING 26

13 Eat honey, my son, for it is good;
    honey from the comb is sweet to your taste.
14 Know also that wisdom is like honey for you:
    If you find it, there is a future hope for you,
    and your hope will not be cut off.

SAYING 27

15 Do not lurk like a thief near the house of the
        righteous,
    do not plunder their dwelling place;
16 for though the righteous fall seven times, they
        rise again,
    but the wicked stumble when calamity
        strikes.

SAYING 28

17 Do not gloat when your enemy falls;
    when they stumble, do not let your heart
        rejoice,

18   or the LORD will see and disapprove
            and turn his wrath away from them.

19   Do not fret because of evildoers
            or be envious of the wicked,
20   for the evildoer has no future hope,
            and the lamp of the wicked will be
                snuffed out.

21   Fear the LORD and the king, my son,
            and do not join with rebellious officials,
22   for those two will send sudden destruction
                on them,
            and who knows what calamities they can
                bring?

FURTHER SAYINGS OF THE WISE

23 These also are sayings of the wise:

        To show partiality in judging is not good:
24   Whoever says to the guilty, "You are
                innocent,"
            will be cursed by peoples and denounced
                by nations.
25   But it will go well with those who convict the
                guilty,
            and rich blessing will come on them.

26   An honest answer
            is like a kiss on the lips.

27   Put your outdoor work in order
          and get your fields ready;
          after that, build your house.

28   Do not testify against your neighbor without
          cause —
          would you use your lips to mislead?
29   Do not say, "I'll do to them as they have done
          to me;
          I'll pay them back for what they did."

30   I went past the field of a sluggard,
          past the vineyard of someone who has no
          sense;
31   thorns had come up everywhere,
          the ground was covered with weeds,
          and the stone wall was in ruins.
32   I applied my heart to what I observed
          and learned a lesson from what I saw:
33   A little sleep, a little slumber,
          a little folding of the hands to rest —
34   and poverty will come on you like a thief
          and scarcity like an armed man.

PROVERBS 25

1 These are more proverbs of Solomon, compiled by
the men of Hezekiah king of Judah:

2   It is the glory of God to conceal a matter;
        to search out a matter is the glory of kings.
3   As the heavens are high and the earth is
        deep,
        so the hearts of kings are unsearchable.

4   Remove the dross from the silver,
        and a silversmith can produce a vessel;
5   remove wicked officials from the king's
        presence,
        and his throne will be established through
        righteousness.

6   Do not exalt yourself in the king's presence,
        and do not claim a place among his great
        men;
7   it is better for him to say to you, "Come up
        here,"
        than for him to humiliate you before his
        nobles.

    What you have seen with your eyes
8   do not bring hastily to court,
    for what will you do in the end
        if your neighbor puts you to shame?

9   If you take your neighbor to court,
         do not betray another's confidence,
10   or the one who hears it may shame you
         and the charge against you will stand.

11   Like apples of gold in settings of silver
         is a ruling rightly given.
12   Like an earring of gold or an ornament of
             fine gold
         is the rebuke of a wise judge to a listening
             ear.

13   Like a snow-cooled drink at harvest time
         is a trustworthy messenger to the one who
             sends him;
         he refreshes the spirit of his master.
14   Like clouds and wind without rain
         is one who boasts of gifts never given.

15   Through patience a ruler can be persuaded,
         and a gentle tongue can break a bone.

16   If you find honey, eat just enough —
         too much of it, and you will vomit.
17   Seldom set foot in your neighbor's house —
         too much of you, and they will hate
             you.

18   Like a club or a sword or a sharp arrow
         is one who gives false testimony against a
             neighbor.
19   Like a broken tooth or a lame foot
         is reliance on the unfaithful in a time of
             trouble.

20 Like one who takes away a garment on a cold
day,
or like vinegar poured on a wound,
is one who sings songs to a heavy heart.

21 If your enemy is hungry, give him food to eat;
if he is thirsty, give him water to drink.
22 In doing this, you will heap burning coals on
his head,
and the Lord will reward you.

23 Like a north wind that brings unexpected rain
is a sly tongue — which provokes a horrified
look.

24 Better to live on a corner of the roof
than share a house with a quarrelsome wife.

25 Like cold water to a weary soul
is good news from a distant land.
26 Like a muddied spring or a polluted well
are the righteous who give way to the
wicked.

27 It is not good to eat too much honey,
nor is it honorable to search out matters that
are too deep.

28 Like a city whose walls are broken through
is a person who lacks self-control.

PROVERBS 26

1   Like snow in summer or rain in harvest,
       honor is not fitting for a fool.
2   Like a fluttering sparrow or a darting
           swallow,
       an undeserved curse does not come to
           rest.
3   A whip for the horse, a bridle for the donkey,
       and a rod for the backs of fools!
4   Do not answer a fool according to his folly,
       or you yourself will be just like him.
5   Answer a fool according to his folly,
       or he will be wise in his own eyes.
6   Sending a message by the hands of a fool
       is like cutting off one's feet or drinking
           poison.
7   Like the useless legs of one who is lame
       is a proverb in the mouth of a fool.
8   Like tying a stone in a sling
       is the giving of honor to a fool.
9   Like a thornbush in a drunkard's hand
       is a proverb in the mouth of a fool.
10 Like an archer who wounds at random
       is one who hires a fool or any passer-by.
11 As a dog returns to its vomit,
       so fools repeat their folly.
12 Do you see a person wise in their own eyes?
       There is more hope for a fool than for them.

13 A sluggard says, "There's a lion in the road,
  a fierce lion roaming the streets!"
14 As a door turns on its hinges,
  so a sluggard turns on his bed.
15 A sluggard buries his hand in the dish;
  he is too lazy to bring it back to his mouth.
16 A sluggard is wiser in his own eyes
  than seven people who answer discreetly.

17 Like one who grabs a stray dog by the ears
  is someone who rushes into a quarrel not
   their own.

18 Like a maniac shooting
  flaming arrows of death
19 is one who deceives their neighbor
  and says, "I was only joking!"

20 Without wood a fire goes out;
  without a gossip a quarrel dies down.
21 As charcoal to embers and as wood to fire,
  so is a quarrelsome person for kindling
   strife.
22 The words of a gossip are like choice morsels;
  they go down to the inmost parts.

23 Like a coating of silver dross on earthenware
  are fervent lips with an evil heart.
24 Enemies disguise themselves with their lips,
  but in their hearts they harbor deceit.
25 Though their speech is charming, do not
   believe them,
  for seven abominations fill their hearts.

26   Their malice may be concealed by deception,
       but their wickedness will be exposed in the
          assembly.
27   Whoever digs a pit will fall into it;
       if someone rolls a stone, it will roll back on
          them.
28   A lying tongue hates those it hurts,
       and a flattering mouth works ruin.

PROVERBS 27

1   Do not boast about tomorrow,
      for you do not know what a day may
        bring.

2   Let someone else praise you, and not your
      own mouth;
      an outsider, and not your own lips.

3   Stone is heavy and sand a burden,
      but a fool's provocation is heavier than
        both.

4   Anger is cruel and fury overwhelming,
      but who can stand before jealousy?

5   Better is open rebuke
      than hidden love.

6   Wounds from a friend can be trusted,
      but an enemy multiplies kisses.

7   One who is full loathes honey from the comb,
      but to the hungry even what is bitter tastes
        sweet.

8   Like a bird that flees its nest
      is anyone who flees from home.

9   Perfume and incense bring joy to the heart,
      and the pleasantness of a friend
      springs from their heartfelt advice.

10   Do not forsake your friend or a friend of your
         family,
             and do not go to your relative's house when
                 disaster strikes you —
             better a neighbor nearby than a relative far
                 away.

11   Be wise, my son, and bring joy to my heart;
             then I can answer anyone who treats me
                 with contempt.

12   The prudent see danger and take refuge,
             but the simple keep going and pay the
                 penalty.

13   Take the garment of one who puts up security
         for a stranger;
             hold it in pledge if it is done for an outsider.

14   If anyone loudly blesses their neighbor early
         in the morning,
             it will be taken as a curse.

15   A quarrelsome wife is like the dripping
             of a leaky roof in a rainstorm;
16   restraining her is like restraining the wind
             or grasping oil with the hand.

17   As iron sharpens iron,
             so one person sharpens another.

18   The one who guards a fig tree will eat its
         fruit,
             and whoever protects their master will
                 be honored.

19 As water reflects the face,
        so one's life reflects the heart.

20 Death and Destruction are never satisfied,
        and neither are human eyes.

21 The crucible for silver and the furnace for gold,
        but people are tested by their praise.

22 Though you grind a fool in a mortar,
        grinding them like grain with a pestle,
        you will not remove their folly from them.

23 Be sure you know the condition of your flocks,
        give careful attention to your herds;
24 for riches do not endure forever,
        and a crown is not secure for all generations.
25 When the hay is removed and new growth
            appears
        and the grass from the hills is gathered in,
26 the lambs will provide you with clothing,
        and the goats with the price of a field.
27 You will have plenty of goats' milk to feed your
            family
        and to nourish your female servants.

PROVERBS 28

1   The wicked flee though no one pursues,
        but the righteous are as bold as a
            lion.

2   When a country is rebellious, it has many
            rulers,
        but a ruler with discernment and knowledge
            maintains order.

3   A ruler who oppresses the poor
        is like a driving rain that leaves no crops.

4   Those who forsake instruction praise the
            wicked,
        but those who heed it resist them.

5   Evildoers do not understand what is right,
        but those who seek the LORD understand
            it fully.

6   Better the poor whose walk is blameless
        than the rich whose ways are perverse.

7   A discerning son heeds instruction,
        but a companion of gluttons disgraces
            his father.

8   Whoever increases wealth by taking interest
            or profit from the poor
        amasses it for another, who will be kind
            to the poor.

9   If anyone turns a deaf ear to my instruction,
          even their prayers are detestable.

10   Whoever leads the upright along an evil path
          will fall into their own trap,
              but the blameless will receive a good
                  inheritance.

11   The rich are wise in their own eyes;
          one who is poor and discerning sees how
              deluded they are.

12   When the righteous triumph, there is great
          elation;
              but when the wicked rise to power, people
                  go into hiding.

13   Whoever conceals their sins does not prosper,
          but the one who confesses and renounces
              them finds mercy.

14   Blessed is the one who always trembles before
          God,
              but whoever hardens their heart falls into
                  trouble.

15   Like a roaring lion or a charging bear
          is a wicked ruler over a helpless people.

16   A tyrannical ruler practices extortion,
          but one who hates ill-gotten gain will enjoy
              a long reign.

17   Anyone tormented by the guilt of murder
          will seek refuge in the grave;
              let no one hold them back.

18   The one whose walk is blameless is kept safe,
         but the one whose ways are perverse will fall
            into the pit.

19   Those who work their land will have abundant
         food,
            but those who chase fantasies will have their
               fill of poverty.

20   A faithful person will be richly blessed,
         but one eager to get rich will not go
            unpunished.

21   To show partiality is not good—
         yet a person will do wrong for a piece of
            bread.

22   The stingy are eager to get rich
         and are unaware that poverty awaits them.

23   Whoever rebukes a person will in the end gain
         favor
            rather than one who has a flattering tongue.

24   Whoever robs their father or mother
         and says, "It's not wrong,"
            is partner to one who destroys.

25   The greedy stir up conflict,
         but those who trust in the LORD will
            prosper.

26   Those who trust in themselves are fools,
         but those who walk in wisdom are kept
            safe.

27   Those who give to the poor will lack nothing,
         but those who close their eyes to them
            receive many curses.

28   When the wicked rise to power, people go into
            hiding;
         but when the wicked perish, the righteous
            thrive.

PROVERBS 29

1   Whoever remains stiff-necked after many
       rebukes
       will suddenly be destroyed — without
       remedy.

2   When the righteous thrive, the people
       rejoice;
       when the wicked rule, the people groan.

3   A man who loves wisdom brings joy to his
       father,
       but a companion of prostitutes squanders
       his wealth.

4   By justice a king gives a country stability,
       but those who are greedy for bribes tear it
       down.

5   Those who flatter their neighbors
       are spreading nets for their feet.

6   Evildoers are snared by their own sin,
       but the righteous shout for joy and are
       glad.

7   The righteous care about justice for the
       poor,
       but the wicked have no such concern.

8   Mockers stir up a city,
       but the wise turn away anger.

9   If a wise person goes to court with a fool,
        the fool rages and scoffs, and there is no
              peace.

10   The bloodthirsty hate a person of integrity
        and seek to kill the upright.

11   Fools give full vent to their rage,
        but the wise bring calm in the end.

12   If a ruler listens to lies,
        all his officials become wicked.

13   The poor and the oppressor have this in
            common:
        The Lord gives sight to the eyes of both.

14   If a king judges the poor with fairness,
        his throne will be established forever.

15   A rod and a reprimand impart wisdom,
        but a child left undisciplined disgraces its
            mother.

16   When the wicked thrive, so does sin,
        but the righteous will see their downfall.

17   Discipline your children, and they will give
            you peace;
        they will bring you the delights you
            desire.

18   Where there is no revelation, people cast
            off restraint;
        but blessed is the one who heeds wisdom's
            instruction.

19 Servants cannot be corrected by mere words;
        though they understand, they will not
            respond.

20 Do you see someone who speaks in haste?
        There is more hope for a fool than for them.

21 A servant pampered from youth
        will turn out to be insolent.

22 An angry person stirs up conflict,
        and a hot-tempered person commits many
            sins.

23 Pride brings a person low,
        but the lowly in spirit gain honor.

24 The accomplices of thieves are their own
            enemies;
        they are put under oath and dare not testify.

25 Fear of man will prove to be a snare,
        but whoever trusts in the Lord is kept safe.

26 Many seek an audience with a ruler,
        but it is from the Lord that one gets justice.

27 The righteous detest the dishonest;
        the wicked detest the upright.

PROVERBS 30

1 The sayings of Agur son of Jakeh — an inspired utterance.

This man's utterance to Ithiel:

"I am weary, God,
   but I can prevail.
2 Surely I am only a brute, not a man;
   I do not have human understanding.
3 I have not learned wisdom,
   nor have I attained to the knowledge of the
      Holy One.
4 Who has gone up to heaven and come down?
   Whose hands have gathered up the wind?
Who has wrapped up the waters in a cloak?
   Who has established all the ends of the
      earth?
What is his name, and what is the name
      of his son?
   Surely you know!

5 "Every word of God is flawless;
   he is a shield to those who take refuge
      in him.
6 Do not add to his words,
   or he will rebuke you and prove you
      a liar.

7   "Two things I ask of you, LORD;
      do not refuse me before I die:
8   Keep falsehood and lies far from me;
      give me neither poverty nor riches,
      but give me only my daily bread.
9   Otherwise, I may have too much and disown
          you
      and say, 'Who is the LORD?'
    Or I may become poor and steal,
      and so dishonor the name of my God.

10   "Do not slander a servant to their master,
      or they will curse you, and you will pay for it.

11   "There are those who curse their fathers
      and do not bless their mothers;
12   those who are pure in their own eyes
      and yet are not cleansed of their filth;
13   those whose eyes are ever so haughty,
      whose glances are so disdainful;
14   those whose teeth are swords
      and whose jaws are set with knives
    to devour the poor from the earth
      and the needy from among mankind.

15   "The leech has two daughters.
      'Give! Give!' they cry.

    "There are three things that are never satisfied,
      four that never say, 'Enough!':
16   the grave, the barren womb,
      land, which is never satisfied with water,
      and fire, which never says, 'Enough!'

17 "The eye that mocks a father,
    that scorns an aged mother,
  will be pecked out by the ravens of the valley,
    will be eaten by the vultures.

18 "There are three things that are too amazing
      for me,
    four that I do not understand:
19 the way of an eagle in the sky,
    the way of a snake on a rock,
  the way of a ship on the high seas,
    and the way of a man with a young
      woman.

20 "This is the way of an adulterous woman:
    She eats and wipes her mouth
    and says, 'I've done nothing wrong.'

21 "Under three things the earth trembles,
    under four it cannot bear up:
22 a servant who becomes king,
    a godless fool who gets plenty to eat,
23 a contemptible woman who gets married,
    and a servant who displaces her mistress.

24 "Four things on earth are small,
    yet they are extremely wise:
25 Ants are creatures of little strength,
    yet they store up their food in the summer;
26 hyraxes are creatures of little power,
    yet they make their home in the crags;
27 locusts have no king,
    yet they advance together in ranks;

28   a lizard can be caught with the hand,
          yet it is found in kings' palaces.

29   "There are three things that are stately in their
          stride,
          four that move with stately bearing:
30   a lion, mighty among beasts,
          who retreats before nothing;
31   a strutting rooster, a he-goat,
          and a king secure against revolt.

32   "If you play the fool and exalt yourself,
          or if you plan evil,
          clap your hand over your mouth!
33   For as churning cream produces butter,
          and as twisting the nose produces blood,
          so stirring up anger produces strife."

PROVERBS 31

1 The sayings of King Lemuel — an inspired utterance his mother taught him.

2 Listen, my son! Listen, son of my womb!
   Listen, my son, the answer to my
       prayers!

3 Do not spend your strength on women,
   your vigor on those who ruin kings.

4 It is not for kings, Lemuel —
   it is not for kings to drink wine,
   not for rulers to crave beer,

5 lest they drink and forget what has been
       decreed,
   and deprive all the oppressed of their
       rights.

6 Let beer be for those who are perishing,
   wine for those who are in anguish!

7 Let them drink and forget their poverty
   and remember their misery no more.

8 Speak up for those who cannot speak for
       themselves,
   for the rights of all who are destitute.

9 Speak up and judge fairly;
   defend the rights of the poor and
       needy.

10   A wife of noble character who can find?
        She is worth far more than rubies.

11   Her husband has full confidence in her
        and lacks nothing of value.

12   She brings him good, not harm,
        all the days of her life.

13   She selects wool and flax
        and works with eager hands.

14   She is like the merchant ships,
        bringing her food from afar.

15   She gets up while it is still night;
        she provides food for her family
        and portions for her female servants.

16   She considers a field and buys it;
        out of her earnings she plants a
            vineyard.

17   She sets about her work vigorously;
        her arms are strong for her tasks.

18   She sees that her trading is profitable,
        and her lamp does not go out at night.

19   In her hand she holds the distaff
        and grasps the spindle with her
            fingers.

20   She opens her arms to the poor
        and extends her hands to the needy.

21   When it snows, she has no fear for her
            household;
        for all of them are clothed in scarlet.

22   She makes coverings for her bed;
        she is clothed in fine linen and purple.

23   Her husband is respected at the city gate,
       where he takes his seat among the elders of
         the land.

24   She makes linen garments and sells them,
       and supplies the merchants with sashes.

25   She is clothed with strength and dignity;
       she can laugh at the days to come.

26   She speaks with wisdom,
       and faithful instruction is on her tongue.

27   She watches over the affairs of her household
       and does not eat the bread of idleness.

28   Her children arise and call her blessed;
       her husband also, and he praises her:

29   "Many women do noble things,
       but you surpass them all."

30   Charm is deceptive, and beauty is fleeting;
       but a woman who fears the LORD is to be
         praised.

31   Honor her for all that her hands have done,
       and let her works bring her praise at the city
         gate.

MY THOUGHTS AND PRAYERS

MY THOUGHTS AND PRAYERS

_____

_____

_____

_____

_____

_____

_____

_____

_____

_____

_____

_____

_____

_____

_____

_____

_____

_____

_____

_____

_____

MY THOUGHTS AND PRAYERS

MY THOUGHTS AND PRAYERS

A NOTE REGARDING THE TYPE

This Bible was set in the Zondervan NIV Typeface, commissioned by Zondervan, a division of HarperCollins Christian Publishing, and designed in Aarhus, Denmark, by Klaus E. Krogh and Heidi Rand Sørensen of 2K/DENMARK. The design takes inspiration from the vision of the New International Version (NIV) to be a modern translation that gives the reader the most accurate Bible text possible, reflects the very best of biblical scholarship, and uses contemporary global English. The designers of the Zondervan NIV Typeface sought to reflect this rich, half-century-old tradition of accuracy, readability, and clarity while also embodying the best advancements in modern Bible typography. The result is a distinctive, open Bible typeface that is uncompromisingly beautiful, clear, readable at any size, and perfectly suited to the New International Version.